Cooking for large numbers

A practical guide to doing your own catering

Judy Robinson

About the Author

Judy Robinson has over 30 years' practical experience in catering for large numbers both in a professional and voluntary capacity. For fifteen years she ran a large banqueting restaurant in south Lincolnshire, organizing functions as varied as wedding receptions, club dinners and funeral teas.

She is now a volunteer cook at a lunch club for elderly people, and also plays a key role in organising dinners and other social events in aid of the local church. This often involves producing a meal for a large number of people without the resources of a professional catering kitchen.

Judy Robinson is an approved tutor in Food Safety for the Chartered Institute of Environmental Health.

First published 2016 by
Sunningdale Press
Langtoft
Lincolnshire PE6 9LB
www.cookingforlargenumbers.com

Illustrations by Shelley Ottaway

A catalogue record for this book is available from the British Library.

ISBN 978-1-5262-0255-0

Contents

Introduction

Doing your own catering for an event like a large family party or club dinner can be both satisfying and enjoyable. You have the flexibility to organise it as you wish, and the cost is likely to be considerably less than booking a hotel or restaurant.

However, for the occasion to be a success, it needs careful planning. If you are a professional caterer with banqueting experience, that is fine. If you are not, this book is for you.

This practical guide is arranged in clearly identified sections, and includes suggestions on:

- choosing a suitable menu
- planning your time
- preparing the room
- calculating quantities and allowing for wastage
- organising the cooking, dishing up, serving and clearing of the meal
- choosing suitable equipment and utensils
- cooking a large Christmas dinner
- serving the drinks.

There are suggested recipes for each course of the meal, including ideas for buffet and salad dishes. Because cooking for large numbers increases the risk of food poisoning, there is also a useful section on food safety. This is followed by some helpful advice on preventing accidents in a busy kitchen.

Hopefully this book will remove some of the stress of catering for large numbers, so whether you are planning an event, cooking the meal, or doing both, you can actually enjoy it.

Recipes

The suggested number of people each recipe serves varies throughout the book. In most cases this is only a guide and will depend on factors such as the type of meal being offered, the ages of the guests and the size of the portions.

The quantities given for each recipe can be easily adjusted to suit the number of people you are catering for.

If a recipe is adapted to serve more people, and larger pans or tins are used, the cooking time may also increase.

Unless it says to the contrary, all recipes in this book are based on produce that is 'prepared' weight. This is the weight that remains after any necessary peeling and trimming.

Soups

Cold starters and hors d'oeuvres

Main course

Choosing the venue and preparing the room

Catering for a special occasion can be quite a challenge. It is even more difficult when the venue is not really suitable. In this situation all you can do is to adapt the menu and seating arrangements to make the best use of what facilities are available. When the venue meets your requirements, catering for a special occasion becomes much easier. From preparing the room to serving the meal, you are well on the way to a successful event.

The location

If possible the venue should be easily accessible and convenient for everyone you plan to invite. In a remote rural location finding the place and getting to it may be difficult. In a busy urban situation, car parking might be limited. You may also need to find suitable overnight accommodation within easy reach of the venue for guests who are not travelling home the same day.

The general impression

If you are planning a winter event, if possible go and see the venue in winter. If you go to view it in summer, it is easy to overlook how it might seem on a cold, wet evening. It is also worth checking if the heating and lighting arrangements are adequate in these conditions. Of course, the reverse is also true. A venue that seems snug and comfortable in winter, may have no windows, and be dark and claustrophobic on a hot summer's day.

If you plan to have photographs taken, it is important to make sure there is somewhere suitable for people to stand, with a pleasant background behind them.

The facilities

It is important that access into the building and to the toilets is suitable for anyone with limited mobility. It is also an advantage if there is somewhere for guests to leave their coats, rather than hanging them on the back of their chairs.

If there are smokers amongst the guests, it is helpful to find out where they can smoke. If you are expecting a number of young children, the venue needs to be suitable for them, possibly having another room available where they can play and let off steam. Hopefully there will be some high chairs or booster seats you can borrow.

The size of the room

It is all too easy to overestimate the size of a function room, especially when it is empty. If possible visit the venue when it is set up for an event similar to the one you are planning. If this is not possible, you may be able to hire or 'borrow' the room for a couple of hours. You can then set out a few tables and chairs to test whether the room is large enough for your needs.

It is important to take into account any space you require for drinks on arrival, or for a bar, or both. If you are planning a buffet, you will need space for the buffet table, and for people to move along it without crowding against guests who are sitting nearby. If you are having dancing later, it might be possible to position the buffet table on the dance floor, and then remove it after the meal.

If there is a disco, they will probably need an area of about 4m x 2m with an electricity supply and room overhead for lighting stands. When there is a group or band playing, or after dinner entertainment, it is worth contacting them beforehand to find out how much space they require. This can then be taken into account when you arrange the tables.

For dancing you will need a reasonable amount of floor space preferably without a carpet. To decide if the dance floor is likely to be large enough for modern dancing, there is a simple guide you can use. Halve the number of guests and then multiply by 4.5 which will give you the necessary floor size in square feet. (Ten square feet are just less than one square metre.)

This formula is based on the general rule that only half the people present will be dancing at the same time. Also it is more fun to dance on a crowded floor than one that is half empty. For ballroom or sequence dancing, or for a barn dance, you will probably need nearly twice as much space.

The kitchen

While looking at the venue, it is also worth checking out the kitchen to reassure yourself that it is suitably equipped for the meal you are planning to serve. It is particularly important to make sure that the cooker is large enough. A shortage of glasses, crockery or cutlery is less of a problem, as you can often hire them, or perhaps borrow from friends.

The tables

For the occasion to be a success you need suitable tables. Lightweight, folding rectangular tables are the most useful and adaptable. They are also very quick and easy to dismantle, or reorganise into less formal seating if you need room for dancing after the meal.

Tables of mixed sizes are difficult to arrange into a formal setting. Wobbly tables are very unsatisfactory, as are tables of different heights, especially when pushed together. When they are covered, the difference in height is not always obvious until someone's glass of wine tips over.

Remember to take into account any tables you may need for drinks on arrival, a bar, disco, buffet or raffle. If you are organising a wedding, Christening or birthday party, you may also need a table for presents, and one on which to display the cake. If there are still some tables to spare and sufficient space in the room, a few small tables placed round the walls, to use as serving tables, will make serving and clearing the meal quicker and easier.

Seating the guests

Each person needs a reasonable amount of space at the table, and room to sit comfortably without being pushed up against the table legs. If possible, for a sit-down meal, allow at least 60cm / 2ft for each place setting. If you are seating a guest on the end of a long narrow table it is important they have enough space to sit and eat in comfort. For a finger buffet where guests are not using a knife and fork, you can usually seat people a little closer together.

Distance between tables

It is important that people have sufficient room to move freely between the tables. Each guest should be able to move back from their place to leave the table, without being squeezed against a wall or colliding into another person's chair.

To quickly check if there is sufficient space between adjacent tables, use two dining chairs, back to back, one at each table. Position each one as if someone is sitting on it, eating a meal. If you can walk easily between the chairs, the tables are far enough apart.

A seating plan

A seating plan will make it clear to the guests which table they are sitting on. It should be displayed in a prominent position near the entrance to the dining room, with the guests' names large enough for most people to read without difficulty. It is also important that the tables are clearly marked to match the seating plan.

A seating plan with name cards will show the guests exactly where they are sitting. Providing everyone turns up, each place will be occupied, so there will be no awkward gaps. Name cards also have the advantage that you can seat people with mobility problems, and children in high chairs, in the most convenient position. You can also put out suitable children's cutlery when you know where they are sitting. Unfortunately, people do not always like name cards, especially when they find themselves seated beside someone they do not care for!

A seating plan without name cards will show the guests which table to sit on, but allows them to choose their own seats on that table.

Without a seating plan, guests are free to sit wherever there is a space. In this situation, it is a good idea to set up about four extra places, so the last people to arrive have a choice of where to sit. This will also help to ensure that couples can sit together. Unfortunately, allowing extra places involves a certain amount of wasted effort, as you are setting up places that will not be used. Also, if it turns out that all the empty places are next to each other, there is a risk that some people could find themselves sitting on a half empty table.

The layout of the room

The layout of the room will depend on the occasion, the size and shape of the room, and what tables are available. When you are working with an assortment of tables, it is best if those of a standard height and width are used for seating the guests. Tables that do not match the others might be suitable for a raffle, or to use as serving tables *(page 10)*.

If there is a celebration cake, it should be displayed in a prominent position in the room, so that everyone can see it being cut. The knife for cutting the cake should be attractive, rather than functional, as it will feature in any photographs of the cake cutting ceremony.

There are several table layouts that are commonly used for larger functions:

Top table and spurs

This layout is often used for wedding receptions and formal dinners. The main guests sit on one side of a long top table, facing the rest of the room. The other guests are seated on both sides of long tables which are positioned at right angles to the top table. It is easier to serve the meal if there is a space between the spur tables and the top table.

At a wedding reception it would be usual for the bride and groom, their close relatives, bridesmaids (unless they are very young and need to be with their parents) and the best man to be seated on the top table.

As well as giving a sense of occasion, this layout has the advantage that no one is sitting with their back to the main guests. With this formal arrangement you would normally have a seating plan with a name card at each place.

Top table and individual tables

This is a variation of the top table and spurs. The top table remains the same, but the other tables are arranged to suit the shape of the room. This arrangement allows you to use different sized tables, including round ones. It is also generally easier for people to come and go from their seats than with a more formal layout, which makes it well suited to a buffet meal.

With this layout you would normally have a seating plan, and the guests on the top table would have name cards. You could either put name cards on the other tables or let guests choose their own seats.

Dinner party layout

In this layout, the tables are arranged individually round the room, with the main table (if there is one) as near the centre as possible. The guests on the main table are seated like the others, around the table, and not just along one side.

This arrangement is a flexible one which can be adapted to suit the occasion and the type of tables that are available. It is particularly suitable for round tables, or when you need space in the centre of the room for a dance floor.

With this layout you can choose whether or not to have a seating plan and name cards, depending on the occasion.

Traditional 'village hall' layout

With this layout, the room is set up with lines of long tables, running from one end to the other. It is most frequently used for a traditional meal such as a harvest supper. You can use either trestle tables or rectangular dining tables, as long as the tables in each line match each other in height and width.

This arrangement is quick and easy to set up before the meal, but can be awkward for those serving at table.

With this layout you can choose whether or not to have a seating plan and name cards, depending on the occasion.

First impressions

A guest's first impression of the room will certainly influence their enjoyment of the occasion. Although during the meal the napkins will be unfolded and the neat lines of chairs broken up, the first sight of the room will be what they remember.

One of the best things about preparing the room yourself is that you can use your imagination to create just the right atmosphere. Table decorations, flowers, balloons and candles are all easily available and can make the most humble room seem very special.

Covering tables with banquet roll

Tables usually need covering so they match each other and look more attractive. While it is possible to hire table linen, it is expensive and unlikely to be an exact fit for the tables you are using. Paper banquet roll, which is obtainable from party shops in various lengths and colours, is an easier and less costly option. Unfortunately, it is not suitable for round tables.

The 50m banquet rolls are usually more economical to buy than shorter ones, and you have less wastage from off-cuts. However, a heavy banquet roll can be awkward to deal with, and if it is made from very thin paper, it can easily tear. The 25m rolls, being lighter, are much easier to handle. Regardless of their length, it is best to choose banquet rolls which have their pattern on the inside, so you can simply unroll them along the table.

Battery operated scissors are ideal for cutting banquet roll. They cut faster than conventional scissors and give a neat edge. If the banquet roll has a clearly visible pattern of lines or squares it is easier to cut it straight.

It is very important that all the dining tables are in the right position before anyone starts covering them. Moving several tables that are pushed together and covered with banquet roll is difficult to do without tearing the paper.

Covering a narrow table

A typical banquet roll is about 120cm / 4ft wide, so will easily cover a narrow table and allow for a suitable overhang down each side.

The table to be covered should be clear of chairs, except for one dining chair without arms. Position this chair at one end of the table, as if someone is going to sit on it to eat a meal.

Place the banquet roll on the table at the other end, so it lies straight across the table, and overlaps the table by the same amount on each side.

Unroll the paper until it overhangs this end of the table by about the same amount as it overlaps on each side.

Keeping the roll straight, unroll it carefully towards the chair, until it reaches the end of the table. Keeping the paper that is covering the table firmly in position with one hand, support the underneath of the roll of paper with the other hand, while allowing it to fall slowly onto the chair.

Cut the paper straight across, so the overhangs at the sides and ends of the table are roughly the same length.

Support the roll of paper as it falls slowly onto the chair

Finally, run your fingers round the table edges and pleat each corner of the paper to neaten it and hold it in place.

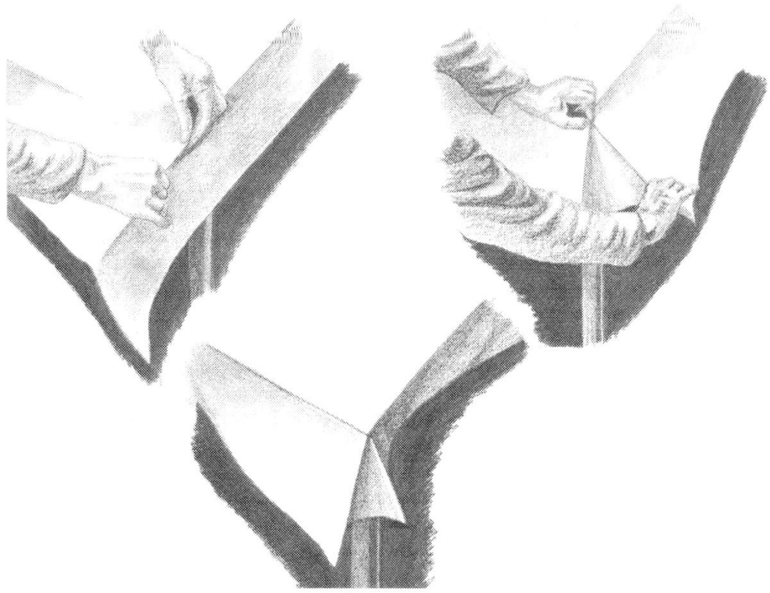

Pleat each corner of the paper to neaten it

Covering a wider table

If the table is much wider than a metre, the banquet roll will probably be too narrow to cover it satisfactorily without using a second piece. In this case you need a slightly different technique.

Place the banquet roll on the table as if covering a narrow table, but position it to one side of the table, so as you unroll it, it overhangs the end and that side of the table by about 20cm / 8in.

Unroll it along the table and onto a chair at the other end, using the same technique as for a narrow table. Cut it across so the overhangs at the ends of the table are a similar length.

Repeat the procedure, this time with the banquet roll overhanging about 20cm / 8in on the other side of the table. (There will be a double thickness of paper down the middle of the table).

If necessary, trim the banquet roll at the ends so they are level. Finish as for a narrow table.

Covering a buffet table or formal top table

A buffet table and a formal top table look more attractive with a 'modesty screen' across the front. If it is a long table, it is much easier if two or three people work together to cover it.

Start as if covering a narrow table, but cut the paper so you only have an overhang of about 10cm / 4in at each end of the table.

Slide this paper down the front of the table until it almost reaches the floor.

Make sure the paper that is still on top of the table is lying flat, and then stick it onto the table top in several places. Use sticky tape or something similar that will not damage the table. Carefully fold back the overhang at each end of the table, neaten it and stick it in place.

Cover the front of a buffet table

Next, cover the table with banquet roll, as if covering a narrow table, but cut it at floor level at each end. Position this piece of banquet roll to give an overlap of about 10cm / 4in at the front of the table.

Crease the paper along the front of the table, so the overlap hangs down like a curtain pelmet, making sure it is level along the length of the table.

Run your fingers round the other three table edges. Tidy the corners of the table by folding the paper neatly, and if necessary sticking the paper in place. It is important that no one can catch their foot in the paper and tear it.

If you are serving a buffet which is two courses or more, it is a good idea to cover the buffet table with an extra layer of banquet roll. Cut it the same length as the table, and do not allow it to overhang the front. It can then be removed quickly after the main course, to leave a clean table for the desserts.

Table covers

These are small paper table cloths which come in various colours and patterns. They are ideal for putting in the centre of a table to give added colour, particularly when you are using white banquet roll. If the table covers and other table decorations complement each other, it will help to produce a coordinated effect throughout the room.

When it is a very informal occasion, you might not need banquet roll underneath the table covers, providing the tables are in reasonable condition.

Place mats

Paper place mats are very useful when you are setting up the tables for a dinner, as you can use them to mark out where each person is sitting. You can also use them as a guide when putting out the cutlery, to make sure each knife and fork is in the right place.

If you are not using place mats, but want to make sure the cutlery at each place setting is in the right position, an A4 sheet of paper makes a useful guide.

Napkins

There are so many colours and patterns of paper napkin that it is not difficult to find one to complement the other table decorations. Some napkins are more suitable for informal parties, while others are sophisticated enough for a wedding or special dinner.

For a sit-down meal, a 40cm, 3 ply napkin is a good choice. It is large enough to be practical, and thick enough to mop up spills. It is also strong enough to support itself when folded into a different shape. If you are preparing the tables for a large party, it is best to avoid complicated napkin folds that require a lot of patience and take ages to do. The napkin fold illustrated is quickly done, looks attractive, and gives added height to the table.

If you fold the napkin without a sharp crease it will look more elegant and be less likely to fall over. To be on the safe side, it is better not to put the folded napkins on the tables until a few hours before the meal.

A paper napkin placed flat in the centre of the table can provide an attractive focus for a candle or small vase of flowers. For the best effect, use a napkin that is either the same design as the table napkins, or one that complements the other colours on the table.

Open the napkin so the inside of the crease runs down the centre

Fold the top corners down to the bottom of the crease and press the point of the napkin to keep the fold in place

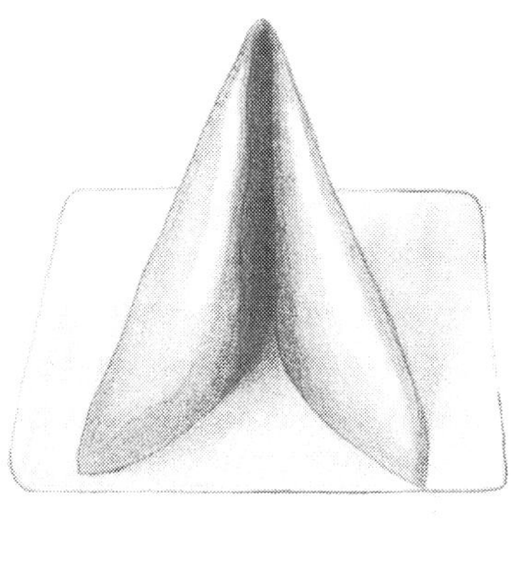

Candles

Candles are excellent at making the tables, and the room, look really special. On the dining tables, candles usually work out cheaper than flowers. They also take up less space, and do not obstruct a person's vision as a large vase of flowers can do.

A plain candle can be transformed by the addition of a pretty candle ring. These are available in various colours and designs to suit most occasions. If you are using candle rings, it is important to remove them before the candles burn down and damage them.

All candles should be securely fixed in their holders. A candle that is slightly wobbly can usually be firmed up by wrapping a small piece of cooking foil around its base. Candles should not be placed near children, and never left unattended. A spark from a candle landing on paper banquet roll can easily result in a fire.

Battery candles are a safer alternative to traditional candles. Although more expensive to buy, if you use candles on a regular basis they could eventually work out cheaper.

Setting the tables

Once a guest sits down, their attention moves from the room as a whole to the table in front of them. It is at this stage that they are likely to notice the condition of the cutlery and glasses, and whether anything is missing from their own place setting.

Ideally, the whole room should have the same pattern of cutlery. If this is not possible, you might at least be able to set each individual table with matching cutlery. The same applies to the glasses and plates. In some situations, when you have to use crockery of different patterns, white doilies can help to provide a coordinated look.

When setting out the cutlery, it is much quicker to do one item at a time across the whole room, rather than setting each place individually. For example, you might start by setting out all the large knives, then the dessert spoons, and so on until the place settings are all done. It is easier and quicker to arrange the cutlery if the chairs are not already in position round the tables.

When setting a place, any cutlery for the first course should be put on the outside of the main course knife and fork. If the dessert spoon and fork are put across the top of the place setting they are easy to identify. The side knife can rest on the side plate, to the left of the place setting.

Once the room is finished, it is a good idea to walk around the tables and quickly check that each place setting is correct. Then the chairs can be put in position, with the front edge of each seat in line with the overhang of the tablecloth. If you are using long tables, the chairs should form straight lines along the sides.

How long will it take?

Preparing a room for a large wedding or dinner is a lengthy business, and it is very easy to underestimate how long it might take. Trying to prepare a room under time pressure is stressful. Knowing that the guests are due to arrive, whether you are ready or not, makes the situation worse.

As a rough guide, it could take two people nearly three hours to arrange the room, cover the tables, and set the places for a formal 3-course dinner for sixty people.

If the room is available the day before the event, the preparations can be far more relaxed. Not only is there less time pressure, but also less risk of interruption by people making last minute changes to the seating plan, or coming round to check on the menu, and so on. Getting the room ready the day before gives you time before the wedding or dinner to concentrate on any finishing touches, and make sure nothing important has been forgotten.

Planning the meal

The type of meal you decide to serve, and whether to choose a buffet or sit-down meal, will depend on the occasion, the guests and the time of year. Other factors, such as the kitchen facilities and what help is available, will also influence the choice of menu.

It can be stressful cooking for a large number of people, particularly if you do not have much previous experience. In this situation, it is far better to provide a simple meal that is well cooked and presented, than try to be more ambitious with the menu and risk disaster.

Buffets

Children and teenagers usually prefer a buffet. It is less structured than a sit-down meal and offers more choice of dishes. Also, at a buffet, people can move away from their own table and talk to their friends in a different part of the room.

A finger buffet is ideal for a Christening or 18th birthday party, especially if you can leave it out for a while so people can help themselves as they wish. It is also a good choice if you are providing the refreshments after a funeral, especially if you are not sure how many people you are catering for, and what time they might arrive. In this situation, it is probably best to offer a simple buffet that looks attractive and is quick to replenish, accompanied by plenty of tea and coffee.

If you are providing a main meal for a large number of people, a buffet is often easier than a sit-down meal. However, you have to prepare more food than the guests are likely to eat, and it also takes up more space, as you need room for the buffet table and a free area in front of it for people to move about.

A meal of three courses and coffee that is served entirely as a buffet can be tedious for the guests. One option is to serve the starter and coffee at the table, and the main course and dessert as a buffet. Or, for the main course, put a selection of platters on the dining tables for people to help themselves.

Sit-down meals

Elderly people usually prefer a sit-down meal. Coping with a buffet can be difficult if you have poor eyesight, or use a walking stick. Elderly people also tend to prefer lunches to evening dinners, so they can get home before dark. This is especially true for those who are having to drive to the venue.

A sit-down meal usually involves more cooking than a buffet, but is quicker to serve. It requires careful planning, and producing a hot meal for a large number of people and making sure it is ready on time, can be a real challenge.

At a large dinner, it is quite usual to serve a set meal. Guests do not have a choice of dishes, so serving the meal is quite straightforward. You can also estimate fairly accurately how much food to prepare, though it is worth allowing a few extra portions for unexpected guests, or in case there is an accident with someone's meal.

Even with a set meal, there should still be a vegetarian option, and it is also useful to have a simple alternative to the starter and dessert. Chilled fruit juice and ice cream are suitable choices, being quick to prepare and serve.

If you are giving the guests a choice of two or three dishes, there needs to be plenty of each. If they have made their selection beforehand, you can plan accordingly, which makes it easier. Unfortunately, people sometimes forget what they have chosen, or change their minds at the last minute. It helps to prevent a muddle if there is a written record of everyone's choice. When there is a formal seating plan, you may be able to write each guest's menu choice on the inside of their name card.

When there is a choice of dishes, it is helpful for the guests if there are menus on each table. For a set meal or a buffet, this is less important, and one large menu prominently displayed is an acceptable alternative.

Menu checklist

The cooker and refrigerator
Are they large enough to cope with the chosen meal?
This is crucial – you can easily borrow a few extra plates but not another cooker!

The crockery and cutlery
Is there enough? Is it suitable?
You can use a dinner plate for egg mayonnaise – but not for soup!

If plates need to be 'recycled' during the meal, someone has to be available to wash them up. Newly washed-up plates are usually warm, which is ideal for hot puddings, but not so good for cold desserts or cheese.

Saucepans, tins and bowls
Are they adequate in size and quantity?
You can soon run out of space on the hob if you have to use two small pans for each vegetable rather than one large one.

It is important not to make the mistake of 'double booking' roasting tins or dishes. This can easily happen. For example, you have decided to make cottage pie for the main course and apple crumble for pudding – but forgotten that they both need the same tins!

What gadgets are needed
Are they up to the job?
It is a tedious business whipping up cream for six dozen trifles with a tiny, hand held whisk.

How much help, time and space are available
Have you enough people to help prepare, cook and serve the meal, and enough time in which to do it? If you are wanting to serve a cold starter, is there sufficient space in the kitchen to lay out all the dishes?

Planning your time

With most lunches and dinners you have a fairly clear idea of when people are likely to arrive and at what time you need to serve the meal. As a rule, elderly guests tend to arrive promptly, and younger people are more likely to be late.

Generally speaking, the more people you are catering for, the longer it takes to prepare and cook the meal. A large pan of frozen vegetables may take nearly an hour to come to the boil. In the oven, large dishes of food take longer to cook than smaller ones. If the oven is overloaded, regardless of the size of the dishes, everything will take longer to cook.

When organising an evening dinner, it is less tiring and stressful if some of the food can be prepared in the morning. With a large lunch it is usually necessary to prepare some of the vegetables the day before.

Making a time plan

Before starting any kitchen work, it is helpful to write down all the jobs that have to be done, along with notes on quantities and timings. This helps to ensure that nothing important is forgotten and is particularly useful when there are several people involved in the preparation and cooking of the meal.

Depending on the situation, this time plan can either be a few rough jottings, or a comprehensive list of instructions. If you regularly cater for large numbers, it is helpful to keep your favourite recipes, with notes on quantities and cooking times, in a folder for future reference.

Calculating how long a meal might last can be difficult. As a guide, a sit-down three course meal and coffee for about 75 people will last between 1½ and 2 hours. A 'full meal' buffet will take at least as long to serve and eat, but a finger buffet will usually be quicker.

Sample time plan

The following example of a time plan is based around an evening meal for forty people being held in a village hall. The kitchen at the hall is reasonably well equipped, with a large gas cooker, a refrigerator, freezer and microwave. It does not have a bain marie to keep food hot.

In this example, the shopping has already been done and taken to the venue. Most of the preparation will be done in the morning, with people coming back to the hall from about 4.30pm to start cooking the meal.

There is a seating plan for the dinner, and four tables with ten guests on each.

The sample time plan is in four parts:
The first part confirms the occasion, the number of guests, the time of the meal and the menu.
The second part lists the morning work.
The third part gives the instructions for cooking the meal.
The fourth part lists the various jobs that need to be done during the evening while the meal is cooking.

BOWLS CLUB DINNER

40 guests inc 2 vegetarians (2 cooked vegetarian pasta dishes in fridge)

Eating 7.30pm

egg mayonnaise + rolls and butter
braised pork chop with mushrooms and onions
baked potato, red cabbage, broad beans
profiteroles with chocolate sauce
coffee or tea

MORNING WORK

hard boil and shell eggs - do about 45 to give a few spare -need 40
wash and spin all lettuces
prepare and wash all cress
wash parsley, make 40 sprigs + few extra
(leave all these covered in fridge)

wash both cucumbers
wash tomatoes, remove stalks

dishes of butter (use saucers) – do 8 + 4 spare (2 per table)
leave in fridge

trim and wash chops – brown on both sides in frying pan and leave in covered container in bottom of fridge

thinly slice onion – need 1.6kg - cover
thinly slice mushrooms – need 1.6 kg – cover

wash potatoes for baking – need 50 large ones – leave on flat tins

Red cabbage
thinly slice 4 onions – weigh them
thinly slice enough red cabbage to give 2.8kg (including onion)
put about 2cm orange juice (from carton) in pan + 4 tbls sugar
add onion and cabbage mixture, stir well - cover and leave

make profiteroles for 50. Cool on racks, cover with clean tea towels

fill water boiler and kettle
prepare coffee cups, milk jugs, sugar bowls (4 trays of 10)
count out 40 dessert plates (egg mayonnaise) and
40 pudding bowls (profiteroles)

put 40 large plates on the hot tray

EVENING WORK - Eating 7.30pm

4.30 ish kettle and water boiler on
oven on mark 4
chops in roasting tins, (use 4 tins) cover with onions and mushrooms
score potatoes
take vegetarian pasta dishes out of fridge
switch on hot tray to warm plates

when kettle boils make stock from chicken cubes & pour over chops to just cover the onions and mushrooms. Cover each tin with foil.

5pm - chops in (lower shelves)
potatoes in (upper shelves)

DON'T FORGET TO ROTATE PLATES!

6pm - turn chops and potatoes

6.15pm start assembling starters (garnish each one with 3 wedges tomato, 3 slices cucumber, parsley sprig, sprinkle of cress)
prepare garnish for 2 vegetarian pasta dishes at the same time

6.45pm cabbage on - stir from time to time (when cooked keep hot on very low heat)
beans on - in freezer – need 2.8kg (when cooked strain and keep hot in a covered colander over simmering water)

7.15pm check chops are cooked (80° C min) strain off stock.
check potatoes. (If chops and potatoes both done then lower oven temperature to keep them hot.)

make gravy to pour over chops – need about 3.4ltr / 6pt
(use stock, water and chicken granules)

heat vegetarian pasta dishes in microwave, min. temp. 72° C
keep hot in oven

just before service – sprinkle paprika on egg mayonnaise

OTHER EVENING JOBS

First job *make mayonnaise sauce in 2 large measuring jugs –*
each jug - 500ml mayonnaise, 50ml salad cream, 50ml milk -
cover them

finish profiteroles: slit them, whip cream stiffly - (need about 1.4ltr - 2 ½pt) - fill them

make chocolate sauce for 50 – use Pyrex bowl in microwave, leave covered

bread rolls in baskets – 2 per table / milk in jugs for coffee / re-boil water for coffee

paprika ready for sprinkling

during main course dish up profiteroles and warm up chocolate sauce

Serving and clearing

This chapter applies mainly to sit-down meals. There is more information in Buffets, page 102, and After dinner coffee, page 112.

A well-cooked meal will be even more enjoyable if it is served in a friendly and efficient manner. To achieve this, the service has to be planned as carefully as the preparation and cooking of the meal.

Suitable clothing

It looks more professional and helps the guests if the people serving at table can be easily identified. For informal occasions, a plain white or coloured apron is acceptable. For more formal dinners, the traditional black skirt or trousers with a white shirt is ideal and easy to organise, as most people have something suitable hanging in the wardrobe. From a food safety aspect it is important that the waiters have a high standard of personal hygiene, and wear suitable clothing made from smooth, washable material. Long hair should be tied back to prevent any loose hair from falling into the food.

Carrying plates

It is quicker and looks more professional if the waiters can carry three plates, rather than just one in each hand. To carry two dinner plates in one hand, you need to support one plate above the other, holding the top plate clear of the food on the bottom plate. One method of doing this is to rest the bottom plate on the first three fingers of your outstretched hand, with the thumb and little finger gripping it firmly from above. Then support the top plate on the base of your palm, and on your thumb and little finger.

When putting the plates down for the guests, put the single plate down first, and then use that hand to lift off the top plate and finally the bottom one.

Serving the meal

For the service to go smoothly you need plenty of help. At a sit-down meal with several courses, it is usually suggested that you have one waiter for every ten to twelve guests. You also need enough people in the kitchen for dishing up. In addition, you might need someone to welcome guests at the door, and if necessary, explain about the arrangements for drinks and where they can leave their coats.

When it is a large dinner with lots of tables it is very easy to get in a muddle. This is less likely if the tables are numbered, and each waiter is responsible for their own particular table, or tables. Displaying a list of who is responsible for each table can be a useful reminder.

It is also helpful if someone feels able to take on the role of head waiter to liaise between the organiser, the other people serving, and the kitchen. They can also keep an eye on the tables and help deal with any problems that arise.

If there are people having vegetarian dishes or special meals, it saves time if someone can find out beforehand where they are sitting. When it is a set meal, it is usually better to take out these dishes after other people on the table have been served. This also applies to the dessert course, especially if the alternative is an attractive ice cream.

When there are young children present, it is a good idea to ask about their needs before you start serving the meal. If you are likely to be catering for young children on a regular basis, it is worth keeping a small stock of children's bowls, beakers and cutlery.

The top table (or main table) should be served first, starting with the most important guests, who are usually seated in the middle. Sometimes with a formal top table the guests sit in a line along one side. People sitting like this should always be served from behind, and not have their food pushed across the table from the front. If there are spur tables coming off the top table, the ones that are nearest the centre of the top table should be served next, starting with people at the top table end.

Once you start serving a table, it should be done as quickly as possible so everyone around the table can begin eating at more or less the same time. When there is a choice of menu, those having cold dishes should be served first. This applies to each course, and helps to ensure that hot dishes have as short a time as possible to cool down before being eaten. When all the tables have been served, one or two waiters should stay in the dining room in case the guests need anything more.

If there are speeches after the meal, the head waiter or another responsible person should remain in the dining room until they have finished. It is usually a good idea if the other waiters leave the dining room at this point, so guests are not tempted to disrupt the speeches by requesting more coffee or drinks.

Serving the first course

Shortly before the meal, jugs of water, and rolls and butter can be put on the tables. When grace is being said, or there are other formalities before the meal, the first course should not be served until these are over and people have sat down. If there are no formalities before the meal, the first course can be served as soon as everyone is seated.

Serving cold starters

The starters should not be put on the tables before the guests arrive. People coming into the dining room will wonder how long their starter has been sitting there, and may even worry about its freshness.

When the starters have been prepared, it is a good idea to take a quick look at one and decide from which angle it looks best. All the starters can then be served with their most attractive side facing the guests.

Cold starters are normally carried out to the tables on trays, but unless there are serving tables, lifting the dishes off the trays can sometimes be difficult. One way is for waiters to work in pairs, with one waiter holding a tray, while the other lifts the dishes off. It is not the quickest method, but preferable to having a tray of dishes dropped on the floor.

Serving soup

Hot soup can be difficult to carry safely from the kitchen to the table. Soup plates with a wide rim are fairly easy to hold. Round bowls are more difficult. The easiest and safest way to carry a round bowl of hot soup is either to put it on a tray, or on a small plate with a napkin or doily under the bowl to prevent it slipping.

Sometimes a guest may be too busy talking to notice their soup arriving. When this happens, it is important to attract their attention before putting the bowl down. This also applies to any other hot dishes you might be serving.

Serving the main course

Sauces, such as cranberry or horseradish, should be put on the tables before the main course is served. If the vegetables are being served in dishes, they should be taken to the table just before, or at the same time as the plates. With large tables, it is usually best if two or more waiters work together to get the meal out quickly so people can start eating while the food is still hot.

Serving desserts

Most desserts can be served in a similar way to cold starters. Jugs of cream or custard should be taken to the table either just before, or at the same time as the desserts.

Serving cheeseboards

Each guest should be given a plate and knife before the cheeseboards are put out. They can then start helping themselves as soon as the cheese and biscuits are on the table. This is usually a good time to serve coffee. If there are after dinner speeches, the cheeseboards could be left on the tables until they are over.

Clearing the meal

To be correct, a table should not be cleared of plates until everyone on it has finished eating. If it is a formal dinner, the top table should be cleared first. When clearing plates, it is usually easier to collect the cleanest ones first, and leave any that still have food on them until last. Sometimes there might be a guest who is taking a long time to eat their meal. If you need to start clearing the plates from their table before they have finished, begin by taking them from the opposite end to where they are sitting.

At a large dinner, it can take a while to sort out bits and pieces like butter dishes and salt and pepper pots that have been cleared from the tables and taken back to the kitchen. It is quicker and easier if similar items have been collected together on the same tray. This system is easier to organise if one or two waiters take a tray and clear all the butter dishes, one or two clear all the salt and pepper pots, and so on.

Clearing the first course

Rolls and butter are normally cleared away after the first course, unless the main course is a salad. If the menu includes baked potatoes or a cheeseboard, you could leave the butter on the tables. Side plates can either be removed after the first course, or left until after the main course.

Clearing the main course

When most people have finished eating, anything that is no longer needed, like vegetable dishes, can be cleared away. If the side plates are still on the tables, they can also be removed. When the menu includes a cheeseboard, the salt and pepper pots can be left until later.

Before serving the dessert course, it is a good plan to quickly check that all the tables have been properly cleared, and replace any dessert cutlery that has been used during the main course.

Clearing the last course

If people are leaving their tables straight after the meal, clearing them is quite straightforward, and you can usually make an unobtrusive start while they are still sitting at their places. Unless you are in a hurry to get cleared, table covers and any floral decorations should remain in place until everyone has left.

When people are not leaving straight after the meal, but staying at their tables, it is important that the tables remain as tidy as possible. Napkins, empty bottles and glasses, crumpled menus and odd pieces of cutlery should all be removed.

Soups

Home-made soup served with a crusty roll or fresh bread is a very popular starter. Producing a large quantity of soup is not usually a great deal more work than making just a few portions. Whether you are making soup for six or sixty, there are a similar number of utensils, boards and bowls to wash. If time is short, packets or tins can be used instead of some of the fresh ingredients. This will cut down the work without spoiling the flavour.

Although soup takes longer to serve than a cold starter, it is often an easier option. This is particularly true in a small kitchen, as plated starters take up much more space than a soup pan. However, although a soup pan will not clutter the work surface, it does use up space on top of the cooker. This can sometimes be a problem, especially if the soup pan is large and the cooker small.

Freezing home-made soup

Most home-made soup, including all the recipes in this book, can be made ahead and frozen, which saves work on the day. It is important to allow sufficient time for frozen soup to thaw and heat up. It may take a large pan of soup over an hour to heat through from cold, and a thick soup can bubble on the top while underneath it is still only lukewarm. Stirring the soup from time to time will help it to heat through evenly.

Checking quantities

When making a large quantity of soup, it is easier to use just one or two big pans than several small ones.

Whether using large or small pans, it is important to keep them covered while the soup is cooking, or too much liquid will be lost through evaporation. Soup needs constant checking, particularly when it is about to come to the boil. As soon as it is left unattended, the chances are it will boil over.

If the soup has to be liquidised, it provides a good opportunity to measure the volume. Any shortfall can be rectified by adding a little more stock.

If you are distracted while making the soup, especially when adding stock to the pan, it is very easy to make a mistake with the quantities. One way to make sure you have enough soup is to use a measuring stick. Firstly, decide what quantity of soup you plan to make in that particular pan. Then, using a measuring jug, pour the same amount of water into the empty pan. Take a long wooden spoon or rolling pin and hold it upright in the pan. Make a mark on it just above the water level. This mark gives an idea of how much soup is needed, although it is always better to make a few extra portions to allow for unexpected guests or spillages.

If you regularly make large quantities of soup, it can be useful to mark the spoon or rolling pin with a scale, for example, 20, 30, 40 portions. It is important that this measuring stick is always used in the same sized pan, or the calculations will go madly awry.

This measuring stick can also be used just before dishing up, to check there is enough soup for the number of guests.

Sampling and seasoning the soup

It is safer to wait until the soup has been made, and you can sample the finished product, before adding any extra seasoning. Sampling the soup can be a problem in itself, as your sense of taste becomes less sensitive after trying several spoonfuls of hot soup. It is a good idea to call on someone else to give a second opinion if you are struggling to improve the flavour of a large pan of soup.

If the soup is a little bland try adding some stock cubes, along with a good shake of pepper. Adding the stock cubes directly to the soup, even if they are crumbled in, can sometimes result in dark specks floating on top. One way to avoid this is to dissolve the stock cubes in a small quantity of soup that has been poured into a bowl or jug. You can then make sure they are properly dissolved before tipping the soup back into the pan.

Portion control

Soup is usually served in portions that vary between 140ml / ¼pt and 280ml / ½pt, depending on the recipe, the occasion, and the size of the soup bowls.

It is important to decide how much soup to give each person before dishing up, or you can easily run short. The easiest method of portion control is to use a ladle of the same capacity as the portion size. This method is particularly helpful when you are dishing up into bowls of various shapes and sizes. When two people are dishing up, their ladles should be the same size, so that everyone gets a similar portion.

Small ladles that need filling twice will slow down the dishing up. If you have to use a ladle that is much larger than the portion size, it is helpful to find out how much it holds before starting to dish up. You can then estimate how full it should be for each portion.

Dishing up soup

Soup can be slow to dish up, especially if there is a fiddly garnish to add to each portion. If you regularly serve large quantities of soup, it is worth getting some extra ladles so you can have two serving points, with two people dishing up at each.

Before dishing up, the soup pan and correct number of bowls should be put in a convenient position for both the people dishing up, and those serving at table. If the soup bowls are going to be carried out on plates or trays, these also need to be close at hand.

Providing everything is correctly positioned, it should be possible for the people dishing up to quickly add a simple garnish to each bowl of soup.

Garnishes for soup

Most soups look more attractive with a contrasting garnish. This can be as simple as a pinch of chopped parsley or a few croutons. Freshly chopped parsley tends to stick to your fingers, but if it is left to dry for a while on a chopping board or plate, it is much easier to sprinkle. A swirl of cream gives soup a sophisticated look. The cream should be at room temperature or slightly warm. Use a small jug with a good spout to pour a little swirl of cream on top of the soup.

Farmhouse vegetable soup

A bowl of this wholesome soup is the perfect starter on a cold winter's day.

Makes 5.5ltr / 10pt (approx). Serves about 20 at 280ml / ½pt each.

2.1kg / 4lb 12oz mixture of finely chopped onions, turnips, leeks, celery and carrots
500g / 1lb 2oz finely chopped new potatoes
4ltr / 7pt well flavoured vegetable stock
7.5ml / 1 level dessertspoon mixed herbs
salt and pepper (as required)

Method

Place all the vegetables in a pan, add the stock and herbs.
Cover the pan, bring to the boil and simmer until the vegetables are soft, about 45 min.
Leave to cool for about 30 min.

Liquidise some of the soup to make it thicker.
Reheat the soup and season to taste.

Variations on the recipe

Small quantities of peas, broad beans, sweetcorn kernels, chopped green beans and mushrooms could also be included in the weight. This recipe can be easily converted into a meat and vegetable soup, by substituting some finely chopped pieces of cooked beef, chicken or turkey, for the same weight of vegetables, and using meat stock. If the pieces of meat are added before cooking the soup, they will soften and give it some extra flavour.

Cream of tomato soup

This delicious soup has a depth of flavour and texture not often found in bought tomato soup.

Makes 5.5ltr / 10pt (approx). Serves about 20 at 280ml / ½pt each.

50g / 2oz butter or margarine
100g / 3½oz flour (plain or self-raising)
100g / 3½oz roughly chopped lean unsmoked bacon
900g / 2lb roughly chopped onions
900g / 2lb roughly chopped carrots
4ltr / 7pt meat or vegetable stock
375g / 13oz tomato purée* (approx)
280ml / ½pt single cream
5ml / 1 level teaspoon mixed herbs
salt and pepper (as required)

*** This recipe is based on tomato purée which is described as 'double concentrate'.**

Method
Melt the butter or margarine in a pan.
Add the vegetables and bacon, cover the pan and cook gently for about 10 min.
Add the flour and cook slowly for about 2 min, stirring well.
Gradually stir in the tomato purée, mixed herbs and about half the stock.
Cover the pan, bring to the boil and cook gently until the vegetables are very soft, about 1 hr.
Leave to cool for about 30 min.

Liquidise until smooth then add the rest of the stock.
Pour the cream into a bowl and add about the same amount of soup.
Stir well and return the mixture to the pan.
Reheat the soup and season to taste, adding more tomato purée if necessary.

Cream of mushroom soup

This classic soup is always popular and perfect for any occasion.

Makes 5.5ltr / 10pt (approx). Serves about 20 at 280ml / ½pt each.

50g / 2oz butter or margarine
100g / 3½oz flour (plain or self-raising)
1.75kg / 3lb 14oz mushrooms
225g / 8oz roughly chopped onions
225g / 8oz roughly chopped leeks
225g / 8oz roughly chopped celery
3.4ltr / 6pt chicken or vegetable stock
425ml / ¾pt single cream
5ml / 1 level teaspoon mixed herbs
salt and pepper (as required)

Method
Melt the butter or margarine in a pan.
Add the onions, leeks and celery, cover the pan and cook gently for about 10 min.
Add the flour and cook slowly for about 2 min, stirring well.
Gradually stir in about 1.1kg / 2lb 8oz of mushrooms, the mixed herbs and about 2.8ltr / 5pt of the stock.
Cover the pan, bring to the boil and cook gently until the vegetables are very soft, about 1 hr.
Leave to cool for about 30 min.

Meanwhile, finely chop the remainder of the mushrooms.
Put them in a smaller pan with the rest of the stock.
Cover and cook gently until soft, about 30 min.
Leave on one side.
Liquidise the large pan of soup until smooth.
Pour the cream into a bowl and add about the same amount of soup.
Stir well and return the mixture to the pan.
Add the finely chopped mushrooms and stock from the smaller pan.
Reheat the soup and season to taste.

If a smoother soup is preferred, cook all the mushrooms together in the 3.4ltr / 6pt of stock.
Liquidise the soup thoroughly, then add the cream as before.

Cream of celery soup

This recipe gives a smooth, creamy soup with a delicious fresh flavour.

Makes 5.5ltr / 10pt (approx). Serves about 20 at 280ml / ½pt each.

50g / 2oz butter or margarine
100g / 3½oz flour (plain or self-raising)
2kg / 4lb 8oz roughly chopped celery
250g / 9oz roughly chopped onions
250g / 9oz roughly chopped leeks
3ltr / 5½pt chicken or vegetable stock
550ml / 1pt single cream
5ml / 1 level teaspoon mixed herbs
salt and pepper (as required)

Method
Melt the butter or margarine in a pan.
Add the vegetables, cover the pan and cook gently for about 10 min.
Add the flour and cook slowly for about 2 min, stirring well.
Gradually stir in the mixed herbs and about half the stock.
Cover the pan, bring to the boil and cook gently until the vegetables are very soft, about 1 hr.
Leave to cool for about 30 min.

Liquidise until very smooth then add the rest of the stock.
Pour the cream into a bowl and add about the same amount of soup.
Stir well and return the mixture to the pan.
Reheat the soup and season to taste.

Minestrone soup

This interesting soup is so filling it is almost a meal in itself.

Makes 5.5ltr / 10pt (approx). Serves about 20 at 280ml / ½pt each.

50g / 2oz butter or margarine
100g / 3½oz flour (plain or self-raising)
900g /2lb mixture of finely chopped onions, leeks, celery, carrots, turnips and cabbage
85g / 3oz chopped green beans (fresh or frozen)
225g / 8oz finely chopped new potatoes
85g / 3oz peas (fresh or frozen)
85g / 3oz spaghetti
3.7ltr / 6½pt meat or vegetable stock
100g / 3½oz tomato purée*
3 cloves garlic, crushed
7.5ml / 1 level dessertspoon mixed herbs
800g / 1lb 12oz tinned chopped tomatoes
400g / 14oz tinned red kidney beans (undrained weight)
salt and pepper (as required)

*** This recipe is based on tomato purée which is described as 'double concentrate'.**

Method

Melt the butter or margarine in a pan.
Add the 900g / 2lb of mixed vegetables, cover the pan and cook gently for about 10 min.
Add the flour and cook slowly for about 2 min, stirring well.
Gradually stir in the mixed herbs and stock.
Cover the pan, bring to the boil and cook gently for 20 min.
Break the spaghetti into small pieces about 2cm / ¾in long and add to the pan along with the green beans, potatoes, peas, tomato purée and garlic.
Simmer in the covered pan until everything is cooked, about 20 min.
Add the red kidney beans and tomatoes with the liquid from the tins.
Stir well and season to taste.

Potato and onion soup

A homely soup which is filling and warming, and simple to prepare.

Makes 5.5ltr / 10pt (approx). Serves about 20 at 280ml / ½pt each.

50g / 2oz butter or margarine
1.4kg / 3lb 2oz roughly chopped onions
450g / 1lb roughly chopped lean bacon
1.6kg / 3lb 9oz peeled and roughly chopped potatoes
3.7ltr / 6½pt well flavoured beef or chicken stock
15ml / 1 level tablespoon finely chopped fresh parsley
7.5ml / 1 level dessertspoon paprika
½ teaspoon pepper
salt and extra pepper (as required)

Method
Melt the butter or margarine in a pan.
Add the onion and bacon, cover the pan and cook gently for about 10 min.
Add the potatoes, paprika, parsley, pepper and stock.
Cover the pan, bring to the boil and cook gently until the potatoes are very soft, about 1 hr.
Leave to cool for about 30 min.

Liquidise until the soup is fairly smooth but still has tiny pieces of bacon and potato in it.
Reheat the soup and season to taste.

Variations on the recipe
Leeks can be used instead of onions to give potato and leek soup.

Carrot and parsnip soup

This is a hearty soup with a delicious combination of flavours.

Makes 5.5ltr / 10pt (approx). Serves about 20 at 280ml / ½pt each.

1.1kg / 2lb 8oz roughly chopped carrots
500g / 1lb 2oz peeled and roughly chopped potatoes
750g / 1lb 10oz roughly chopped parsnips
550g / 1lb 4oz roughly chopped onions
3.4ltr / 6pt well flavoured beef stock
550ml / 1pt milk
salt and pepper (as required)

Method
Put all the vegetables in a pan with about half the stock.
Cover the pan, bring to the boil and cook gently until the vegetables are very soft, about 1 hr.
Leave to cool for about 30 min.

Liquidise until fairly smooth, then add the milk and the rest of the stock.
Reheat the soup and season to taste.

Broccoli and Stilton soup

There is just a hint of Stilton in this sophisticated soup.

Makes 5.5ltr / 10pts (approx). Serves about 20 at 280ml / ½pt each.

50g / 2oz butter or margarine
100g / 3½oz flour (plain or self-raising)
450g / 1lb roughly chopped onions
450g / 1lb roughly chopped leeks
700g / 1lb 8oz roughly chopped celery
550g / 1lb 4oz florets of broccoli (with very little stalk)
2.5ltr / 4½pt chicken or vegetable stock
225g / 8oz grated Stilton
1.4ltr / 2½pt milk
salt and pepper (as required)

Method
Melt the butter or margarine in a pan.
Add the onions, leeks and celery, cover the pan and cook gently for about 10 min.
Add the broccoli and cook for another 10 min.
Add the flour and cook slowly for about 2 min, stirring well.
Gradually stir in the stock.
Cover the pan, bring to the boil and cook gently until the vegetables are very soft, about 1 hr.
Remove from the heat, add the grated Stilton and stir until it has melted.
Leave to cool for about 30 min.

Liquidise until smooth then add the milk.
Reheat the soup and season to taste.

Cold starters and hors d'oeuvres

Some sections of Salads, page 78, are also relevant to cold starters and hors d'oeuvres.

A cold starter usually means no soup pan. This is good news if the top of the cooker is small and there are several large pans of vegetables needing the space. A cold starter also means cold plates, and these are easier to carry than bowls of hot soup.

Attractive starters and hors d'oeuvres make an impressive beginning to a special meal, but even if most of the preparation has been done in advance, they usually require a certain amount of last minute work. When large numbers are involved, it can be quite stressful trying to get all the starters prepared and ready on time.

In a hot kitchen, the starters and any salad garnish can soon dry out. When the kitchen is very busy, it can also be difficult to find sufficient space to prepare, assemble and garnish all the starters. It is a great help if most of the work can be done ahead. The kitchen will be cooler, there will be more free space to work in and less time pressure. Also, any problems concerning the quantity or quality of the produce are usually found during the initial preparation. If it is done in advance you will probably still have time to put things right before the meal.

Any high risk food, ie high protein moist food, that has been prepared in advance must be kept under refrigeration until shortly before the meal, to minimise the risk of food poisoning.

Preparing salad garnish

Salad garnish that has been prepared in advance must be stored carefully to keep it fresh. Plastic boxes, casserole dishes with lids, or even saucepans, are all suitable as storage containers. Ideally, the containers of prepared salad should be kept in the refrigerator. If there is not enough space and they have to stay in a warm place, covering the containers with cold, wet tea towels will help to keep them cool.

Celery – trim the ends, wash, then slice or chop. If leaving the stalks whole, just trim the ends and wash. Long stalks can be wrapped in cling film for temporary storage.

Cress – cut with scissors, put in a sieve, wash under cold running water and shake well to drain.

Cucumber – wash and preferably leave whole as sliced cucumber dries out very quickly. If you do have to slice it in advance, push the slices together and wrap the sliced cucumber in cling film. Put the wrapped cucumber in a sealed container which has been rinsed out with cold water. This will help to prevent the cucumber from drying out.

Lettuce – wash, then remove excess water with a salad spinner, or by patting with a clean tea towel. Cut or tear the leaves as you need them.

Orange and lemon slices (or wedges) – wash the whole fruit, slice it, and remove the pips.

Parsley – trim, put in a sieve, wash gently under cold running water, shake well to drain.

Radishes – trim and wash. If they are sliced in advance, be sure to keep them well covered, as they quickly dry out.

Spring onions – trim, wash and slice.

Tomatoes – these tend to fall apart if they are cut up in advance, so it is usually preferable to just wash them and then leave them to drain.

Watercress – trim, wash and leave in a little water in a covered container. Put it on the plates at the last minute, as it quickly dries out.

Garnishing starters

The garnish of a cold starter is usually part of the dish itself, adding substance to the main food item, while at the same time making it look more appetising. With seafood dishes, it is usual to include a lemon slice or wedge.

The garnish should complement the food in terms of taste and colour. For example, a slice of liver pâté would look well served with lettuce, cucumber and parsley, with a few slices of red tomato to brighten it up, and a sprinkle of cress over the top. This garnish would also provide a pleasant contrast to the richness of the pâté.

A more delicate starter, like a prawn cocktail, can be easily overwhelmed by too much garnish. A starter of this type needs only a simple decoration with a subtle use of colour.

'Plating up' (arranging food on the plates)

It is helpful to have one starter prepared ahead of the rest, to use as a model for the others. This should ensure that all the dishes look the same, and no pieces of garnish are omitted.

Plating up a large number of starters is a time consuming task, especially if they contain a substantial salad garnish. It is quicker if they can be done in a special preparation area.

This preparation area should include a chopping board, a selection of knives, and several small bowls containing the relevant food items. These bowls can be replenished from the main storage containers. The preparation area should also have an empty bowl to use as a table top waste bin.

Rather than assembling each starter individually from beginning to end, it is quicker to use a production line system. If there are enough trays to take all the starter dishes it makes the task of plating up much quicker and easier.

Begin by putting a tray of starter dishes down on the preparation area. Then, working evenly across the dishes, gradually assemble the starters from the food items taken in turn from the small bowls. For example, to plate up a tray of seafood starters, you might begin by placing some lettuce on each dish, then the fish, then maybe a slice of lemon, continuing like this, until all the starters on the tray are finished.

If the starters contain high risk food items, like cold meat, fish or egg, the finished trays of dishes should be put in a refrigerator until it is time to serve the meal. If the shelves in the refrigerator have enough space between them, you might be able to stand tins or small containers on some of them to support extra trays. If there is not sufficient space for all the trays, the plating up of the high risk items should be left until just before the meal.

Mixed hors d'oeuvres

A variety of interesting hors d'oeuvres can be made by combining two or more food items with an attractive salad garnish. If time is short, there are plenty of ready prepared foods available in jars or tins, or at the delicatessen counter.

In these mixed hors d'oeuvres, it is important to choose the food items carefully. It is usually better not to mix fish and meat, or two very moist foods on the same plate. The whole arrangement should be pleasing to look at, with flavours and textures that complement each other.

Some of the more substantial items on the following list could also be served on their own, as a single hors d'oeuvre.

Suggestions for mixed hors d'oeuvres

Thinly sliced beef, turkey, chicken or ham
Sliced salami and smoked sausage
Fresh, tinned or smoked salmon
Tinned sardines and tuna fish
Smoked trout or mackerel
Pickled herrings
Anchovy fillets
Prawns, whole and shelled
Cockles and mussels
Crab and lobster meat
Stuffed eggs*
Hard boiled eggs, in halves or quarters
Cottage cheese
Firm cheese, diced or grated
Filled tomatoes*
Party mushrooms*
Celery boats filled with cream cheese*

*The recipes for these dishes can be found at the end of this chapter.

Suggested salad garnish for one mixed hors d'oeuvre

1 large or 2 small lettuce leaves
3 wedges of tomato
3 slices of cucumber
parsley sprig
cress to sprinkle
1 slice or wedge of lemon (for a seafood hors d'oeuvre)

Suggested salad garnish for 10 mixed hors d'oeuvres

1 round lettuce
350g / 12oz tomatoes
½ a cucumber
few sprigs of parsley
1 tub cress
2 lemons (for seafood hors d'oeuvres)

Suggested salad garnish for 50 mixed hors d'oeuvres

5/6 round lettuces (approx 1.25kg / 2lb 12oz total weight)
1.7kg / 3lb 12oz tomatoes
2 long cucumbers
50g / 2oz parsley
5 tubs cress
7 lemons (for seafood hors d'oeuvres)

Mixed hors d'oeuvre platters

Mixed hors d'oeuvre platters make an interesting change from traditional starters. Guests are given an empty plate each and help themselves from platters on the table. These mixed hors d'oeuvre platters look most attractive, and at dinners they help to break the ice as people talk to each other while they pass them round the table. If there is not enough room on the dining table for all the platters, the mixed hors d'oeuvres can be served from a side table, like a buffet.

The platters should provide plenty of choice and allow for personal preferences, offering a good selection of food, including meat, fish, eggs or cheese and one or two interesting salads. Because people are helping themselves, you can include some more unusual items amongst the hors d'oeuvres. A row of salad garnish across a platter can separate the different types of food.

Checking quantities

If the hors d'oeuvres are served on platters it can be difficult to calculate how much to prepare. For the first course at a dinner, a selection of about six hors d'oeuvres should provide enough variety. Each person should be able to take a little of everything, without completely emptying the platters. Obviously, some items will be more popular than others.

One way of doing a quick check on portion sizes is to pretend you are a guest. Take a plate, and help yourself to a little of each hors d'oeuvre including one or two salad items and some garnish. The portion on the plate should be roughly the same as a generous sized starter.

Ideas for salad and garnish on mixed hors d'oeuvre platters

Potato salad
Rice salad
Coleslaw
Sweetcorn kernels
Asparagus spears
Lettuce (different varieties)
Red, yellow and green peppers
Celery
Tomatoes
Cucumber
Radishes
Spring onions
Gherkins
Parsley and cress
Lemon slices or wedges (to accompany seafood hors d'oeuvres)
Black or green stoned olives
Pickled onions and walnuts

Prawn cocktail

This popular starter is easy to prepare, looks special and is suitable for any occasion.

Serves 20.

1.4 kg / 3lb 2oz shelled prawns (if using frozen prawns, this is the thawed and drained weight)
800g / 1lb 12oz iceberg lettuce
600ml / just over 1pt prawn cocktail sauce

Suggested garnish
3 lemons
20 whole prawns in their shells
2 tubs cress

Method
Slice or tear the lettuce into small pieces and put some into each prawn cocktail dish.
Divide the shelled prawns between the dishes, piling them up on top of the lettuce.
Spoon about 30ml / 2 tablespoons of sauce over the prawns in each dish.

Both the following sauces make a good topping for prawn cocktail. They are milder than most shop bought sauces, and will not mask the delicate flavour of the prawns. If the sauce is too thick, add a small quantity of thin cream or milk.

Prawn cocktail sauce (1)

Mix together:
425ml / ¾pt shop bought prawn cocktail sauce
175ml / 6fl oz mayonnaise

Prawn cocktail sauce (2)

Put 425ml / ¾pt of mayonnaise into a measuring jug.
Keep adding small amounts of tomato ketchup, cream (single or double) and extra mayonnaise until there is 600ml / just over 1pt in the jug, and you feel that the flavour and consistency are correct.

Garnish the top of each prawn cocktail with a wedge or slice of lemon, a whole prawn and a sprinkle of cress.

Notes on the recipe
If frozen prawns are used, they need adequate time to thaw out. Prawns that are allowed to thaw slowly have a better flavour than those thawed quickly in water. Either way, the prawns must be drained well before use.
Iceberg lettuce is a good variety for prawn cocktail as it stays crisp for quite a while under the prawns and sauce. The suggested quantity of lettuce might be more than you need, depending on the size of the dishes.
The lettuce and prawns can be portioned into the dishes an hour or so before the meal, if there is room in the refrigerator for all the dishes. The sauce can be made ahead, covered and refrigerated.
Prawn cocktail can be easily changed to seafood cocktail by substituting other shellfish, or small pieces of cooked salmon for some of the prawns.

Liver pâté

This is an excellent pâté, and although it takes a while to prepare, it can be made a day or two ahead, and kept under refrigeration until needed. It also freezes well.

Serves about 24.

Use 2 x 2lb loaf tins, (22cm x 12cm x 6cm). Grease the sides and bottom of each tin with a little margarine and cover the bottom with greaseproof paper.

100g / 3½oz margarine
225g / 8oz chopped pork sausage meat
600g / 1lb 5oz chopped pigs liver
375g / 13oz chopped streaky bacon
170g / 6oz soft white breadcrumbs
280ml / ½pt red wine
15ml to 30ml (1 to 2 tablespoons) brandy
225g / 8oz roughly chopped onions
4 crushed cloves garlic
2 large beaten eggs
1 level teaspoon mixed herbs
½ teaspoon mixed spice
pinch of salt and pepper

Suggested garnish
2 to 3 round lettuces
850g / 1lb 14oz tomatoes
1 cucumber
50g / 2oz parsley
2 to 3 tubs cress

Before making the pâté, if time permits, cover the liver with cold milk and leave it in a refrigerator for 48 hours. Then rinse it well. The milk will give the pâté a more subtle flavour.

Method
Melt the margarine in a pan and gently fry the onion, garlic, bacon, liver and sausage meat for 10 min, stirring occasionally.
Add the wine, brandy, herbs, mixed spice and seasoning.
Bring to the boil, cover and simmer for 30 min.
Leave to cool for about 30 min.

Add the beaten eggs.
Purée in a liquidiser until smooth.
Return to the pan and stir in the breadcrumbs.
Place inside the loaf tins.
Cover them with foil and stand them in an ovenproof dish or tin. Pour enough water into the dish to bring it about 2.5cm / 1in up the sides of the loaf tins. Cook at 190°C, 375°F, gas mark 5 for 1 hr.
After cooking, push the foil down and put a weight on top to press down on the pâté until it is cold. A folded tea towel under a heavy book makes a suitable weight.

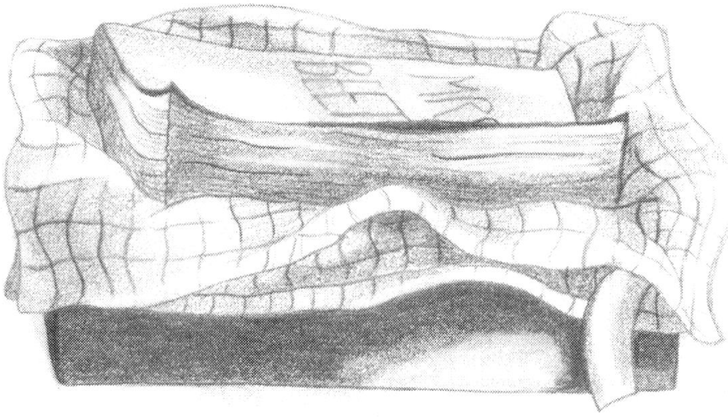

Using a heavy book to press down the pâté

To turn out the pâté, run a knife round the inside of the tin to loosen it, and invert it onto a board.
Peel off the greaseproof paper and cut the pâté into neat slices.
Garnish each portion with lettuce, three wedges of tomato, three slices of cucumber, a parsley sprig and a sprinkling of cress.

Pâté is usually served with a few slices of melba toast. If using bought melba toast, allow about 20g per person, plus some extra in reserve.

Fruit cocktail

This is a delicious fresh tasting starter which, if possible, should be served chilled in small glass dishes.

Fruit cocktail can be made from a combination of any of the following: oranges, grapefruit, melon, pineapple and grapes.

For 10 servings allow approx 1.4kg / 3lb 2oz of prepared fruit, and 140ml / ¼pt of fruit juice.

Preparing the fruit

Oranges and grapefruit – cut across to give two halves and remove the flesh with a grapefruit knife, discarding any white pith.

Melon – cut in half and discard the seeds. Either make melon balls from the flesh, or cut it into chunks with a knife.

Pineapple – remove the skin and cut the fruit into neat chunks, discarding the core.

Grapes – wash the grapes. Small seedless ones can be left whole. Cut large grapes in half and remove any pips.

The fruit can be prepared a few hours in advance, and then stored in separate covered containers until needed. Fruit cocktail is more refreshing if served cold, so if possible the prepared fruit should be kept in a refrigerator. If there is not enough space, draping the containers with cold, wet tea towels will help to keep them cool.

Dishing up fruit cocktail

Drain the fruit and pour the juices into a measuring jug to use later. Take a container of fruit and portion a little into each dish, until it is all used up. Do the same with the fruit in the other containers, so that all the dishes have the same variety of fruit, in similar proportions. Give each fruit cocktail a stir to mix up the fruit.

It is unlikely there will be enough fresh juice for all the cocktails, so you may need to add some orange, pineapple or grapefruit juice from a carton. It is worth making up about 10% more juice than you expect to need, so there is plenty for all the cocktails. Pour about 15ml / 1 tablespoon of juice over each fruit cocktail.

If you are short of suitable dishes, try using grapefruit skins. They are unbreakable and disposable - ideal for outdoor catering! For an attractive effect, cut the grapefruit round the middle with a zig-zag line. Remove the flesh and refill each half with fruit cocktail. Grapefruit skins often leak a little juice, so it is best to stand them on a small dish, and not add the juice until the last minute. Each half grapefruit will hold about 120g / 4oz of fruit cocktail.

Dishing up fruit cocktail

How the fruit cocktails are decorated will depend on the type of fruit and the shape of the dishes. A decoration to give height and a contrast of colour is often the most suitable.

When calculating the proportions of fruit for the cocktail, you need to take into account any fruit being used as a decoration. For example, an orange and melon cocktail that is decorated with a twist of orange, needs to be made with a higher proportion of melon than orange, or it could seem rather 'orange heavy'.

If there is space in the refrigerator for the dishes, the fruit can be portioned out several hours before the meal, saving time later on.

Tinned pineapple chunks in natural juice make an acceptable substitute for fresh pineapple, especially if used as part of a mixed fruit cocktail. Putting the tins in the refrigerator the day before they are needed will ensure the pineapple, and its juice, is chilled ready for use.

Melon boats

This starter is fun to design and make and is ideal for a summer dinner or wedding.

Whole melons weighing about 1.5kg / 3lb 6oz will make 6 boats.
Whole melons weighing about 900g / 2lb will make 4 boats.

To make the melon boats

It is easier to cut the melon into even sized wedges if you score one end of it first, as a guide.

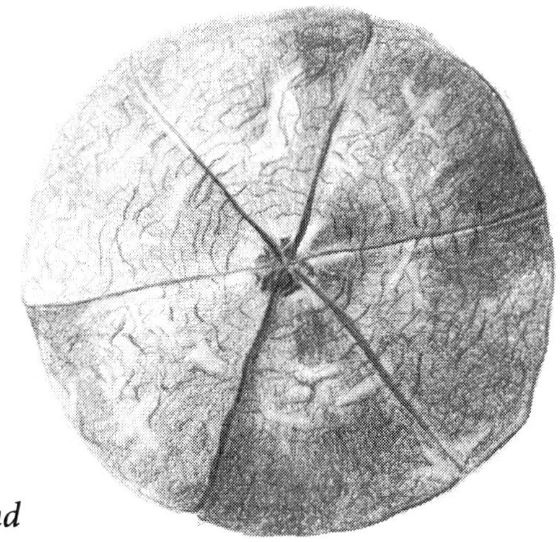

Score the melon at one end

Cut the melon into long wedges, and remove the pips.
If a wedge is wobbly, remove a small piece of skin from underneath, so it does not tip over.
Cut between the skin and the fruit of each wedge, to detach the fruit, but leave it in place.

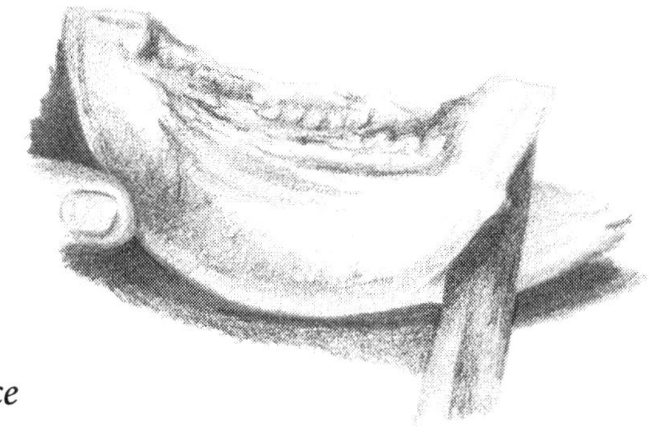

Detach the fruit but leave it in place

Make cuts across the wedge, about 1cm / ½in apart, all the way from one end to the other.

If the melon wedge is a suitable shape, these narrow strips of melon can be pushed out sideways, alternating the sides, to give the impression of oars.

To make an edible sail, push a cocktail stick through opposite edges of an orange slice.
Put a glacé cherry onto one end of the stick, and push the other end of the stick into the melon boat.
Decorate around the base of the mast with sliced fruit, for example, pieces of kiwi fruit, strawberry and pineapple.
To give the melon a more interesting flavour, you could slide some very thin slices of stem ginger between the 'oars'.

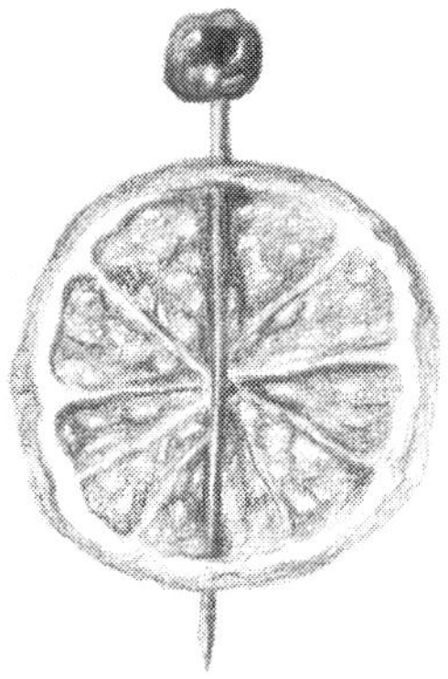

An edible sail

Using a napkin as a sail

Notes on the recipe
The cutting of the melons can be done in advance. The sails can also be made ahead and secured onto the masts. After cutting, cover the melon wedges and orange sails with cling film to keep them moist.
A medium sized orange will give six or seven slices suitable for sails.
There are about 20 glacé cherries in 1 x 100g tub.

A sail for a melon boat can also be made from a small but good quality paper napkin. Cut a napkin into four quarters, and fold each piece twice, to give a triangular sail. These paper sails will need longer masts, which can be made from wooden skewers or spills, trimmed to a suitable length. The sails can be secured onto the masts with a dab of glue.
For Christmas, or a special celebration like a wedding, it can be fun to make the sails to suit the occasion.

Egg mayonnaise

Egg mayonnaise is a popular starter, and looks very attractive if it is well presented.

Serves 20.

20 eggs, hard boiled and shelled
2 round lettuces
500g / 1lb 2oz mayonnaise
50g / 2oz salad cream
50ml / 2fl oz milk

Suggested garnish
700g / 1lb 8oz tomatoes
1 cucumber
40g / 1½oz parsley
2 tubs cress
paprika (very little is needed, 15g / ½oz is enough for nearly 100 eggs)

Method

Thoroughly mix together the mayonnaise, salad cream and milk to make a sauce.
Put a leaf or two of lettuce on each plate, slightly to one side.
Cut each egg in half lengthways.
Place two halves, side by side, cut sides down, in the middle of each plate.
Using a dessert spoon, carefully pour a spoonful of sauce over each egg half, so that it forms a smooth coating.
If the sauce is too thick, add a little more milk.

Garnish each portion around the sides with three wedges of tomato, three slices of cucumber, a parsley sprig and a sprinkling of cress.

Just before serving, sprinkle the paprika over the egg.
If using a tub of paprika with a perforated top, sprinkle it straight from the tub.
Otherwise put about ½ teaspoon of paprika into a tiny, fine meshed sieve which is supported over a cup. Hold the sieve over the egg and gently tap it on one side to release a fine sprinkling of paprika.

Notes on the recipe

Some of the eggs may crack open during cooking, so it is a good idea to boil about 10% more than you need. They will be difficult to shell unless they are cooled quickly after boiling, and with a large number of eggs, this can be a problem. One way is to tip them straight into a large container of very cold water, and keep changing the water as it warms up. Or you can tip them out of the pan into a large colander, and run cold water over them until they are cold. It will help if you can crack their shells as they go into cold water.

The eggs can be hard boiled and shelled several hours in advance, and put in the refrigerator. The sauce can also be made ahead, covered and refrigerated. The paprika should be sprinkled on shortly before service. If done earlier, it will run into the sauce and look most unattractive.

Because of the amount of work that has to be done shortly before service, egg mayonnaise is not the easiest starter to make in large numbers.

Smoked mackerel mousse

This recipe is easy to make, and although the mousse is quite rich, the flavour is pleasant without being too strong. This recipe can be made in fairy cake tins, or muffin tins, instead of special moulds. It can also be served as a pâté to spread on melba toast.

Serves about 30.

700g / 1lb 8oz skinned smoked mackerel fillets
4 eggs, hard boiled and shelled
300g / 10½oz mayonnaise
25g / 1oz gelatine powder*
140ml / ¼pt vegetable stock
140ml / ¼pt double cream
50g / 2oz margarine
50g / 2oz flour (plain or self raising)
550ml / 1pt milk
pinch of salt, pepper and mace

*** If using a different type of gelatine, you need enough to set 2pt of liquid.**

Suggested garnish
3 round lettuces
1kg / 2lb 4oz tomatoes
1½ small cucumbers, or 1 long cucumber
50g / 2oz parsley
3 tubs cress
4 lemons

Method
Grease the required number of small moulds.
Make a white sauce from the margarine, flour and milk, leave to cool.
Flake the fish, discarding any small bones.
Chop the hard boiled eggs, then mash well into the fish.
Add the white sauce, mayonnaise and seasoning, stirring well.
Thoroughly dissolve the gelatine in the stock and stir into the mixture.
Lightly whip the cream and fold it in.
Spoon the fish mousse into the moulds, smoothing the top of the mixture.
Leave to set in a refrigerator.

To turn out the mousse, first run a flexible knife blade around the inside of the mould to loosen the mixture.
Then ease the mousse out of its mould, or invert the mould over a board, and shake well. If the mousse does not come out, dip the bottom of the mould briefly in very hot water.
Once the mousse has been removed from the mould, it can be smoothed over with a knife dipped in hot water.

Garnish each portion with lettuce, three wedges of tomato, three slices of cucumber, a lemon wedge or slice, a parsley sprig and a sprinkling of cress.

Notes on the recipe

Smoked mackerel mousse can be made a day or two ahead and refrigerated, and it also freezes well, either in its moulds, or after turning out. If it is frozen in its moulds, it is easier to turn out while still partly frozen. Leave it to finish thawing on a board or plate.

Stuffed eggs

Makes about 20.

Method

Hard boil and shell 10 eggs.
Cut them in half lengthways.
Remove the yolks, put them in a bowl with any whites that have broken, and add about 50g / 2oz of salad cream or mayonnaise.
Mash them together.
Keep adding a little more salad cream or mayonnaise until the mixture is very smooth, and of a piping consistency.
Using a large star nozzle, pipe the mixture back into the empty egg whites.

Notes on the recipe

If there is not enough mixture to fill all the egg whites, empty ones can be filled with something different, for example prawns or grated cheese.
If several egg whites break, you may end up with too much filling. It can be used to fill tomato halves, celery boats, or sandwiches.
If numbers are critical, it is worth boiling some extra eggs to allow for wastage. There are tips on hard boiling a large number of eggs on page 50.

Filled tomatoes

Makes 20, using 10 firm, red tomatoes, weighing about 70g / 2½oz each.

Method

With a thin serrated knife, cut a zig-zag round the centre of each tomato and pull the two halves apart. Scoop out the flesh and pips, and fill with something of a contrasting colour, for example:

Prawns in mayonnaise – 280g / 10oz of shelled prawns (if using frozen prawns, this is the thawed and drained weight) mixed with 140g / 5oz of mayonnaise.

Cottage cheese – 425g / 15oz.

Sweetcorn kernels – 250g / 9oz drained weight.

Party mushrooms

Makes 25.

25 firm mushrooms, about 5cm / 2in across
850ml / 1½pt vegetable stock (approx)
200g / 7oz soft cream cheese
small amount of mayonnaise or double cream (if needed)
pinch of salt and pepper

Method
Remove the mushroom stalks as close to the caps as possible.
Put both caps and stalks in a pan and cover with stock.
Bring to the boil and simmer for 10 min.
Lift them out and leave to drain on a wire rack.
When cool, put the mushroom caps upside down on a board or plate.
Mix the cream cheese with the seasoning, and if necessary add a little mayonnaise or double cream to give a piping consistency.
Using a large star nozzle, pipe a swirl of cheese where each stalk came from.
Push the stalks back in, and serve as upside down mushrooms.

Celery boats filled with cream cheese

Makes 25.

5 sticks of celery
200g / 7oz cream cheese
small amount of mayonnaise

Method
Trim and wash the celery.
Slice a thin strip off the underside of each stalk, from one end to the other, so the boats will sit firmly without rolling about.
Mix the cream cheese with the seasoning, and if necessary add a little mayonnaise or double cream to give a piping consistency.
Using a large star nozzle, pipe the cheese into the celery, either straight along the groove of the stalk, or in a zig zag pattern from side to side.
Cut each stalk into five pieces.
Either leave the stalks plain or decorate them with a sprinkling of paprika or finely chopped parsley.

Main course

The main course, as well as being the most important part of the meal, is usually the most difficult to organise, especially without a bain marie or hot cupboard to keep food hot. Everything has to be ready at more or less the same time, and then served quickly before it has a chance to cool down.

The main course can be served either as a plated meal, where all the food is dished up on the plates, or as a semi-plated meal, where just the meat or fish is put on the plates, and the vegetables are served in dishes for guests to help themselves. A plated meal is quicker both to serve and eat, and involves fewer dishes, and therefore less washing up. A semi-plated meal is generally more popular with guests as it gives them a choice of vegetables. It is also easier to offer second helpings of vegetables if they are served in dishes.

With a semi-plated meal, you need to decide beforehand how many vegetable dishes to put on each table. It is more convenient for the guests if not more than six of them have to share one vegetable dish or gravy boat. Vegetable dishes do not need lids. They clutter the table and make it more difficult for people to serve themselves.

Serving versus dishing up – getting the balance right

To keep everything flowing smoothly there needs to be the right balance between the number of people waiting at table and those in the kitchen dishing up. If there are too many waiters and too few in the kitchen, the waiters will be queueing for plates. If there are too many people in the kitchen and too few waiters, the food on the plates will be cooling off before it reaches the guests.

As an example, at a dinner for sixty guests, where the main course is roast beef, you might have five or six waiters serving at table, and four people in the kitchen working like this:

one dishing up beef
one dishing up Yorkshire puddings and roast potatoes (both coming straight from the oven)
one dishing up vegetables
one dishing up gravy and mashed or new potatoes.

If you have large numbers to cater for, it will help the people dishing up if there is someone else in the kitchen to fetch things they need, like extra plates, or tins of roast potatoes from the oven. This will enable the dishing up to continue without interruption, which in turn will speed up the service of the meal.

It is also helpful if someone can start washing up the first course while the main course is being served.

Dishing up the main course

Before starting to dish up, make sure all the plates, dishes and utensils are close at hand.

Plated meals are best dished up like a production line. The plates are stacked near the first person in the line, who takes a plate and serves up some meat or fish. The plate is then passed to the next person, who puts, for example, potatoes on it. This continues down the line until the meal is complete. It is a good idea if the last person in the line checks each meal to make sure nothing is missing and that it is properly presented. The production line should finish where the waiters can conveniently collect the plates and take them to the guests.

The dishing up of a semi-plated meal will vary according to the menu, but should be organised so that the plates of meat or fish for each table, and accompanying dishes of vegetables, are ready at the same time.

Cooking meat

Suitable methods of cooking meat for a large dinner include pot roasting, braising and stewing. Your butcher should be able to give advice on the various cuts of meat and how best to cook them.

The suggested cooking times and quantities in this book are only a guide. If the oven is overloaded with meat and vegetables, everything will take longer to cook.

Pot roasting meat

If possible buy large, boneless joints of meat. There is little wastage with large joints, and they are less likely to dry out than smaller ones. It is quicker and easier to carve a joint if it is boneless. Beef, pork and gammon are simple to cook and carve, and give good sized slices on the plate. Lamb joints, being smaller, are a little more difficult to handle. Chickens, roasted whole, take up a lot of oven space and are slow to carve. If you want to serve poultry, a boneless rolled breast of turkey is a much easier option.

Before cooking a joint, pour about 1cm / ½in of water into the roasting tin. Cover the joint with foil and bring it over the edges of the tin. This will keep the joint moist. Every hour or so during cooking check the temperature of the meat. If necessary, baste it with the liquid from the tin, and turn it round if it is not cooking evenly. If the tin is getting too full of liquid, drain some off. If it is nearly dry, add a little more water.

To prevent food poisoning from undercooked meat, a joint should not be taken from the oven until it has reached a minimum temperature of 75°C and is hot enough to hold that temperature for two minutes in the thickest part of the meat.

Suggested cooking temperatures for roast meat

Beef and gammon 75°C
Lamb and turkey 78°C
Pork 80°C

The cooking time will depend upon the type and quality of the meat, the weight and thickness of the joints, and the oven temperature. As a rough guide, a joint of meat weighing about 3.6kg / 8lb cooked under foil, will probably take between 3 and 4 hrs to cook at 200°C, 400°F, gas mark 6.

Roast beef

Allow about 180g / 6½oz raw meat per serving.
1kg of beef will provide about 5½ servings.
For every 10 servings you need about 1.8kg of beef.
If working in imperial weights, divide the number of servings by five, and double the answer, to find the weight in lb that you need.

A different way of serving roast beef is to provide each table with a joint for one of the guests to carve. Rolled rib is ideal, and a table of ten to twelve is a good size to share a joint of about 3.6kg / 8lb. This is more beef than you would normally allow, but a larger joint looks more impressive and people are likely to want second helpings.

You will need a carving board and a carving knife and fork for each joint. The knife should be sharp, so the meat cuts easily. If the person carving is provided with a striped apron and paper chef's hat, it adds to the sense of occasion!

If there is enough space, put a small 'carving' table near each dining table. Any debris and mess from the carving can then be quickly and easily cleared away, and the dining tables will remain clean and tidy.

Yorkshire puddings

Individual Yorkshire puddings, cooked and frozen, are readily available in the shops, and are the easiest solution for a large dinner. Small puddings are quicker to dish up than large ones which need portioning. If you are making the puddings yourself, it is usually best to get them made and out of the way before it is time to start cooking the meal.

To reheat the puddings, pile them into roasting tins and put them into a moderate oven about half an hour before you need them. Have some spare puddings in case some get flattened, scorched or lost at the back of the oven while they are being reheated.

Roast pork (with rind)

Allow about 225g / 8oz raw meat per serving.
1kg of pork will provide about 4½ servings.
For every 10 servings you need about 2.25kg of pork.
If working in imperial weights, divide the number of servings by two, to find the weight in lb that you need.

It is usually possible to get some crackling on the joint, even if the pork is cooked in water. Start by rubbing plenty of salt into the scored rind. Cook the meat under foil for about an hour. Then cut the foil along the top and fold it back to leave most of the rind uncovered, allowing it to crisp up. The bottom half of the joint should remain under the foil so it keeps moist.

If the rind does not crackle very well you can try cutting it off and cooking it separately in a shallow tin. Put it in the hottest part of the oven about half an hour before you need it. The joint should be covered with some more foil if the rind has been cut away.

At a large dinner, you rarely get enough crackling to give everyone a piece. In this situation, it is sometimes better not to dish up any crackling, and only give it out to individual guests who request it.

Roast pork (without rind)

Allow about 200g / 7oz raw meat per serving.
1kg of rindless pork will provide about 5 servings.
For every 10 servings you need about 2kg of pork.
If working in imperial weights, for every 10 servings you need about 4lb 8oz of pork.

Roast gammon

Allow about 225g / 8oz raw meat per serving.
1kg of gammon will provide about 4½ servings.
For every 10 servings you need about 2.25kg of gammon.
If working in imperial weights, divide the number of servings by two, to find the weight in lb that you need.

The following two-stage system of cooking gammon keeps it moist and removes any excess saltiness.

Put the gammon in a saucepan of cold water and bring to the boil. Simmer for 10 min. Discard the water, bring to the boil again in fresh water, and simmer until the centre of the joint is between 65°C and 70°C. (This is likely to take about 2 hrs for a 3.6kg / 8lb joint.) Remove from the pan, and when cool enough to handle, strip off the skin.

Put the joint in a roasting tin and brush the fat with either melted honey, or brown sugar dissolved in a little hot water. Roast the gammon uncovered in a moderate oven for about 45 min, or until the fat is coloured and the meat is cooked.

Adding a little mustard and cranberry sauce to gravy gives it a slightly piquant flavour which is delicious with roast gammon.

Roast lamb

Allow about 200g / 7oz raw meat per serving.
1kg of lamb will provide about 5 servings.
For every 10 servings you need about 2kg of lamb.
If working in imperial weights, for every 10 servings you need about 4lb 8oz of lamb.

Roast turkey

Rolled boneless breast of turkey is ideal for a large dinner. It is much easier to carve than a whole bird, and there is very little waste. Because it does not contain any brown meat, the portions will all look similar.

Allow about 200g / 7oz raw weight of rolled boneless breast per serving.
1kg of turkey will provide about 5 servings.
For every 10 servings you need about 2kg of turkey.
If working in imperial weights, for every 10 servings you need about 4lb 8oz of turkey.

Chipolata sausages

These are often served as an accompaniment to roast turkey. If you have a large quantity of chipolatas to cook, it is easier to do them in the oven, rather than grill or fry them. Cook them in a single layer in a shallow roasting tin. To prevent them from sticking, cover the bottom of the tin with a little water.

It is a good plan to cook more sausages than you are likely to need, in case some get burnt or fall to the back of the oven, or roll off someone's plate onto the floor!

Stuffing

The packets of dried stuffing to which boiling water is added are very easy to use and give good results, though it is worth buying a reputable brand.

If the stuffing is portioned out before it is cooked, it will ensure that everyone gets the same amount. A portioner (a gadget like an ice cream scoop) makes neat little domes of stuffing that are quick to dish up. A good size for a stuffing portioner is about 5cm / 2in across. Using one this size will probably give fewer portions of stuffing than is suggested on the packet.

These individual portions of stuffing should be cooked in a single layer in a greased dish or tin. If the oven is hot, they should be covered with foil for the first part of the cooking time, to prevent them drying out.

If you are not using a portioner, but making the stuffing in a large tin, it is helpful to mark out the portions with a knife before you dish it up. This will avoid any possibility of the stuffing running out before everyone has been served.

Gravy

As a guide, 550ml / 1pt of gravy will serve about 7 people. For every 10 people allow about 800ml / just under 1½pt of gravy.

Beef or poultry juice taken from the roasting tin and diluted with water makes excellent gravy. The proportions should be about one third meat juice to two thirds water. The juice from pork and lamb is rather fatty, and should not make up more than a quarter of the total volume of the gravy. Stock taken from a stew also makes first class gravy and it does not need to be diluted as much as gravy made from meat juices.

If there is not enough stock for the gravy, the cooking water from the vegetables can be added, or used instead. Potato water is a little starchy, but the water from carrots, peas, beans, broccoli and cauliflower is suitable. It is better not to make the gravy from just one type of vegetable water, as the flavour and colour can be too intrusive.

To make the gravy, put all the measured liquid in a pan, cover it, bring it to the boil and whisk in the correct amount of gravy granules, as suggested on the carton. Chicken gravy granules are usually the most satisfactory, whatever flavour of gravy is being made. Beef gravy granules tend to be rather strong, especially when combined with well flavoured beef stock.

If there is a choice of menu, and you are offering, for example, beef or turkey, it is not necessary to make two types of gravy. If you use a mixture of meat juices you can make a delicious gravy that is suitable for both.

Gravy granules are also very useful for thickening soups and stews and adding flavour at the same time. If they are being added to a pan of light coloured stock it is especially important to dissolve them properly, otherwise some will remain as dark specks floating on the surface. They are easier to dissolve if you add them to a small amount of very hot liquid taken from the pan. Beat them into the liquid with a hand whisk, and when they have dissolved and the liquid is smooth, pour it back into the pan.

Dishing up gravy

If you are dishing up into gravy boats, you can leave the gravy in the pan to keep hot, and ladle it out as required.

If the gravy is being poured over individual portions on the plates, it is much quicker and less messy to use a large jug rather than a ladle. If you have a very large pan of gravy, use a second jug to transfer the gravy from the pan into the pouring jug. This is safer than trying to tip the hot gravy straight out of the pan. It also keeps the pouring jug clean.

Some people do not care for much gravy, so it is usually safer to give everyone a small amount to start with, and offer more when you have finished dishing up.

Braising meat

This is a good method of cooking meat for a large number of people. Having one piece of meat per person makes portion control easier. If possible the pieces of meat should all be a similar size. If time permits, first seal the meat and brown it by frying it on both sides in a little hot fat. Then braise it slowly in a covered dish, with the vegetables and stock or wine.

The braised meat and vegetables usually look more attractive on the plate if they are in a sauce or gravy. This can be made after the meat is cooked, shortly before dishing up. Pour off most of the stock from the tins of cooked meat, and strain it through a sieve. Re-cover the tins and return them to a low oven to keep hot. It is unlikely there will be enough stock, so you will probably need to make some more from stock cubes.

For every 10 servings you need about 700ml / 1¼ pints of stock, which allows 50ml / 2fl oz of sauce per serving with some left in reserve.

Bring the liquid to the boil and thicken it with either chicken gravy granules or white thickening granules, or a mixture of both, depending on the meat and the type of sauce you are making. Tasting the sauce is the only sure way of getting it right!

Dishing up braised meat

A large metal spoon is usually best for dishing up braised meat. Before starting to dish up, it is a good idea to measure out a sample serving of sauce onto an empty plate, to give an idea of how much should be poured over each portion.

When pouring the sauce over the meat, it is quicker and less messy to use a jug rather than a ladle. If the sauce and meat lack colour, a sprinkling of chopped parsley will liven them up.

Braised beef

Normal sized portions are usually between 170g and 180g (6oz and 6½oz). For each person you also need about 40g / 1½oz of thinly sliced onion and 40g / 1½oz of chopped mushrooms.

Put the meat, onions and mushrooms in the roasting dishes or tins, and pour over the stock or a mixture of stock and red wine or beer. Cover the tins with lids or foil and cook in a very moderate oven 170°C, 325°F, gas mark 3, until the meat is tender, about 2½ to 3 hrs.

Braised pork chops

The chops should be trimmed of rind and fat. They can be braised with onions and mushrooms in a similar way to braised beef, although they do not take as long to cook. If you are adding wine, use white rather than red. Chops are also delicious cooked in apple juice, or in a mixture of cider and stock, with double the quantity of onions and without the mushrooms. Apple sauce also makes a tasty addition to the stock when you are braising pork chops.

Braised chicken breasts

Chicken breasts are an easy choice as they are bought as individual portions and do not usually need any trimming. They can be cooked in a similar way to braised beef and pork chops, although they will not take as long to cook as either of these.

Stews and casseroles

A stew is made from cubed meat and vegetables, cooked in stock in a saucepan on top of the stove. It is a good choice of dish if you want to free up the oven for something else. Stirring the stew from time to time while it is cooking will help to prevent the meat at the bottom of the pan overcooking before the rest is tender. A stew is less likely to burn on the bottom if you use a thick based saucepan.

If a stew is cooked as a casserole, in a covered dish in the oven, it is much less likely to burn underneath. However, cooking the meat in a shallow dish makes it harder to thicken up the stock. Dishing up with a ladle can also be difficult out of a shallow dish. Without a ladle, getting each portion the same becomes more difficult.

Portion control can be difficult with stews. If you are worried about the quantity, it is worth checking the number of portions before dishing up. This usually involves ladling the stew into another container, counting as you go. Rather a chore, but at least you will know beforehand if there is not quite enough, and can remedy the situation by giving everyone slightly less.

Beef stew

For every 10 portions allow about 1.75kg / 3lb 15oz of cubed stewing steak, and 750g / 1lb 10oz of chopped vegetables. Onion, carrot, swede, turnip, parsnip, leeks, mushrooms and celery are all suitable.

Put the cubed meat and vegetables in a pan and almost cover with hot stock.
Put a lid on the pan, bring it to the boil and simmer for about 2 hrs, or until the meat is tender.

When the stew is cooked, drain off any stock that is above the meat. It will make excellent gravy. Thicken the stew with either chicken granules (to add more flavour), white thickening granules, or a combination of both.

For accurate portion control, dish up the stew using a 140ml / 5fl oz ladle, filling it for each serving.

Meat pies

Home-made meat pies are very popular, but they use up a lot of oven space and need watching, as they can easily dry out or burn on the bottom and round the edges.

For every 10 portions allow between 1.3kg and 1.6kg (2lb 14oz and 3lb 9oz) of meat, depending on what other ingredients are in the pie. All the dishes should be of a similar depth, between 4cm and 5cm (1½in and 2in).

The meat and vegetables should be cooked first before the pastry is added. If the pies are made in large tins, the pastry in the middle may take longer to cook than the pastry around the sides. If this happens, the sides of the pastry can be covered with foil to stop them cooking any further, while the pastry in the middle of the tin has a chance to catch up.

Portion control and dishing up pies

When cooking a number of pies for a large dinner, it might be necessary to use dishes and tins of different shapes and sizes. This can make portion control difficult, especially when you are trying to dish up quickly and someone else is helping you.

In this situation, it is a good idea to plan ahead while you have time to think. Before putting the pies in the oven, make some rough drawings or notes of what tins you are using and how the various pies should be portioned out. Just before dishing up, mark the top of each pie according to your notes. This will only take a few minutes and will ensure everyone has a similar sized portion.

It can be difficult to cut a round pie into an uneven number of portions, especially when you are in a hurry. This method is worth a try, once you have decided how many portions you want from the pie, and therefore roughly how large they should be:

Make the first cut from the middle to the edge

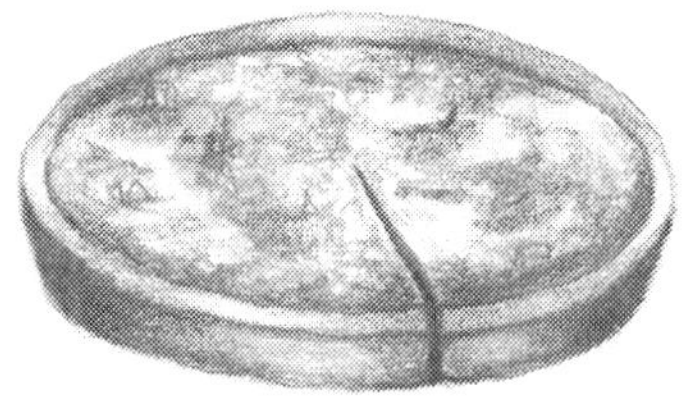

Cut from the middle to the opposite edge, but slightly to one side

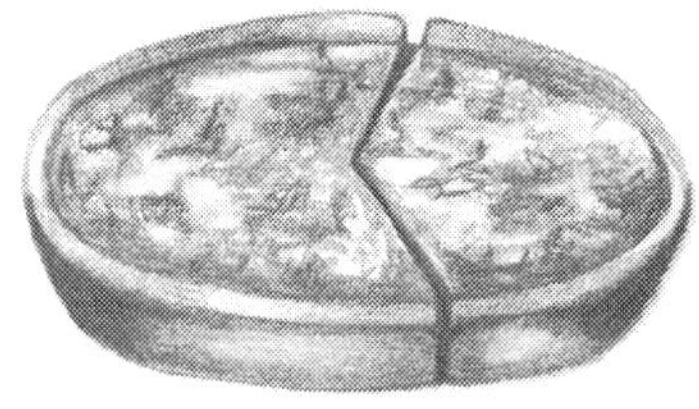

Make another cut a suitable distance away from this second cut, to give the 'odd' portion

Cut each of the two remaining pieces of pie into the same number of portions

This method of cutting a pie can also be used with gateaux, flans, quiche etc.

The utensils for dishing up should be the right shape for the pie. A rectangular server is best for straight sided tins and a pointed pie server for round ones. A large spoon is also useful, as is a damp cloth, as meat pies can be messy to dish up.

Fish as a main course

Individual salmon steaks are probably the best choice if you want to serve fish as a main course. Portion control is easy and they require little preparation. Salmon steaks can either be poached in the oven in a covered tin, or on the hob in a frying pan.

Once they are cooked, salmon steaks can be kept hot for a while in a low oven. Put a little water in the bottom of the tin or dish and cover the pieces of fish with foil so they remain moist. If there are a large number of salmon steaks to keep hot, arrange them in layers, separating each layer with buttered greaseproof paper.

Salmon steaks are delicious served with hollandaise sauce. Packets of hollandaise sauce mix are easy to use, though some have a better flavour than others. The sauce can be made a short while before it is needed and then reheated for service. Put a lid on the pan to prevent a skin forming.

Whether you are pouring hollandaise sauce over each salmon steak, or sending it out in sauce boats, allow about 30ml / 2 tablespoons for each serving, (300ml / just over ½pt for every 10 servings).

Steak and kidney pie

Serves about 22.

3.1kg / 7lb steak and kidney
600g / 1lb 5oz chopped mushrooms
600g / 1lb 5oz mixture of chopped onion and carrot

For this quantity, you need about 1kg / 2lb 4oz of pastry, bought or home-made, or the recipe for quick flaky pastry (page 65).

Method
Put the meat and vegetables in a pan and just cover with stock.
Cover the pan, bring to the boil and simmer until the meat is tender, about 2 hrs.
Strain off the liquid.
Put the meat and vegetable mixture into the pie dishes.
Bring the liquid back to the boil, and thicken with either chicken gravy granules, white thickening granules, or a combination of both, depending on the flavour.
Pour enough thickened stock into the pie dishes to almost cover the meat.
Cover with pastry and cook in a moderately hot oven 200°C, 400°F, gas mark 6 for about 40 min or until the pastry is cooked.

Sausage meat and apple plait

This recipe is simple to make and delicious hot or cold. It can be made the day before and refrigerated, and it also freezes well.

Serves between 6 and 8.

900g / 2lb sausage meat
250g / 9oz peeled and cored apples, eating or cooking
50g / 2oz soft breadcrumbs, white or brown

For this quantity you need about 500g / 1lb 2oz of pastry, bought or home-made, or half the recipe for quick flaky pastry (page 65).

Method

Mix the sausage meat and breadcrumbs together in a bowl.
Coarsely grate the apples and add to the mixture, working it all together.

Roll out the pastry into a rectangle about 46cm x 25cm (18in x 10in). If this length of pastry is too large for the baking sheets, cut it in half to give two smaller squares.

Put a ridge of sausage meat mixture lengthways down the middle of the pastry. Cut the side pieces of pastry into strips and fold them across the top of the sausage meat to resemble a plait.

Brush the tops of the plaits with milk, and bake at 200°C, 400°F, gas mark 6 for about 1 hr, reducing the heat or covering them if they start to get too brown. (The inside of the plaits should be at least 80°C before they are removed from the oven.)

With a metal slice, carefully remove the plaits from the tins. Either serve hot, or leave to cool on a wire rack.

An electric carving knife, or serrated bread knife will make a neat job of slicing these plaits. It does not matter if your plaiting is rather uneven, as it will not show once they are cut up.

The finished plait

Quick flaky pastry

This is an easy recipe which tastes delicious and is very simple to make. Flour the work surface well and handle the pastry carefully when rolling it out as it tends to be rather soft. This pastry should be cooked at about 200°C, 400°F, gas mark 6.

This quantity will make pastry lids for 20 to 25 portions of pie.

225g / 8oz butter
150g / 5½oz margarine
500g / 1lb 2oz plain flour
200ml / 7fl oz boiling water

Method
Cut the butter and margarine into small pieces and place in a bowl.
Pour over the boiling water and stir until the fat is dissolved. If it does not dissolve, warm the liquid.
Add the flour, mix it all together.
Cover the bowl and refrigerate for at least 8 hours.
Take the pastry out of the refrigerator about an hour before it is needed.

Quick chicken sauce

This is a tasty sauce to pour over chicken breasts, and is a useful standby when time is short. It will make 30 portions of sauce at 70ml / 2½fl oz per portion with some left in reserve.

2kg tinned chicken soup
450g / 1lb shop bought mayonnaise
50g / 2oz Madras curry paste (approx)

Stir the soup and mayonnaise together in a pan, and heat the mixture but do not allow it to boil. Add the curry paste gradually so you can adjust the flavour of the sauce. If it is a little too thick add some chicken stock.

Cottage pie

Serves about 22.

3.3kg / 7lb 8oz good quality minced beef
3.5kg / 7lb 14oz peeled and roughly chopped potatoes
900g / 2lb finely chopped onion
1kg / 2lb 4oz tinned chopped tomatoes
6 beef stock cubes (approx)
150g / 5½oz tomato ketchup
little margarine, butter or milk (for mashed potatoes)
little oil for frying

Method
Boil the potatoes until very soft, drain and mash well, adding a little margarine, butter or milk to make a creamy mash.

While the potatoes are cooking, sweat the onions in a little oil in a covered saucepan until they soften, but be careful not to burn them.
Add the minced beef and cook for a few more minutes, stirring all the time.
Add the tinned tomatoes, tomato ketchup and crumbled stock cubes.
Gradually bring everything to the boil, stirring from time to time.
If the mixture seems very dry add a small amount of water.
Simmer until the mince and onions are cooked then strain off any liquid. (It will make excellent gravy.)
Taste the mixture at this stage, and if necessary, add another crumbled stock cube.
Put the mince in the dishes and spread the mashed potato on top.
Use a fork to make ridges in the top of the potato.
Bake in a moderately hot oven 200°C, 400°F, gas mark 6, for about 30 min, or until the meat is hot and the potato is brown and crisp.

Notes on the recipe
As both the beef and potato are already cooked, the oven temperature is not critical, providing the pie is properly heated through.

If the pie is made in large tins, it can take a while for the potato in the middle to brown. One way to speed things up is to put the tin under a grill or use a blow torch.

This recipe can be turned into a minced beef pie, by covering the minced beef with pastry instead of potato. The quantities of pastry will be the same as for steak and kidney pie *(page 63)*.

Chilli con carne

Chilli con carne is usually served with rice or as a filling for baked potato. It is ideal for a hot buffet, being easy to cook, serve and eat. It goes well with a green salad.

Serves about 18.

2.7kg / 6lb good quality minced beef
700g / 1lb 8oz finely chopped onion
700g / 1lb 8oz tinned red kidney beans (drained weight)
1.3kg / 2lb 14oz tinned chopped tomatoes
10ml / 1 rounded dessertspoon ground cumin
10ml / 1 rounded dessertspoon oregano
10ml / 1 rounded dessertspoon paprika
7.5ml / 1 level dessertspoon chilli powder * (approx)
15ml / 1 tablespoon English mustard
30ml / 2 tablespoons soy sauce
2 beef stock cubes
little oil for frying

* It is safer to put in a little less chilli powder to start with, and add some more later if necessary. You cannot take it out!

Method
Put a little oil in a saucepan and fry the onions a short while to soften them.
Add the mince and cook for a few more minutes, stirring all the time.
Add the spices, mustard, soy sauce, crumbled stock cubes and tomatoes.
Stir the mixture well and add a little water if it seems too dry.
Bring to the boil and simmer until the mince and onion are cooked.
Stir in the drained beans.
Heat everything through, and if necessary, add some more chilli powder.
Just before serving, remove a little of the stock if you want a drier mixture.

Dumplings

A comforting addition to a traditonal beef stew, especially on a cold winter's day.

For about 24 dumplings.

450g / 1lb self-raising flour
200g / 7oz beef suet (from a packet)
7.5ml / 1 level dessertspoon baking powder
280ml / ½pt water (approx)
½ teaspoon salt

Method

Sieve the flour, salt and baking powder into a bowl.
Mix in the suet, and gradually add enough water to make a soft dough.
Shape little balls from the mixture, rolling them in flour so they are less sticky.

Put the dumplings in a single layer, either on top of the stew, or in about 4cm to 5cm (1½in to 2in) of boiling stock in a separate pan. Allow space between them so they can expand as they cook, without sticking together.
Cover the pan and boil gently for between 20 and 30 min.

Notes on the recipe

To test if the dumplings are cooked, push a small sharp knife into one. The knife should come out clean, with no mixture sticking to it.
If you are making a large number of dumplings, they will probably have to be made in several batches, which will extend the total cooking time.
Cooked dumplings can be kept hot in a low oven, in a covered tin which has a little stock in the bottom.

Vegetables

The vegetables should be suitable for the menu, the occasion and the time of year. The colour and texture of each vegetable should also be considered, so that the finished meal is attractive on the plate. It is also important to choose vegetables that are easy to keep hot without spoiling, especially when you do not have the benefit of a bain marie.

The exact quantity of vegetables you need for a dinner can be difficult to calculate. The quantities that are suggested in this chapter allow for an average sized portion for each person with a little to spare. At a wedding meal or family occasion with lots of children present, you will need fewer vegetables than at an evening dinner of a similar size.

Preparing vegetables

Most people find it easier to peel potatoes and carrots with a peeler, rather than a knife. Potato peelers vary, not only in their design, but also in the amount of peel they remove. Some are very wasteful, or uncomfortable to use, but unfortunately it is difficult to find out how well a peeler performs without trying it out.

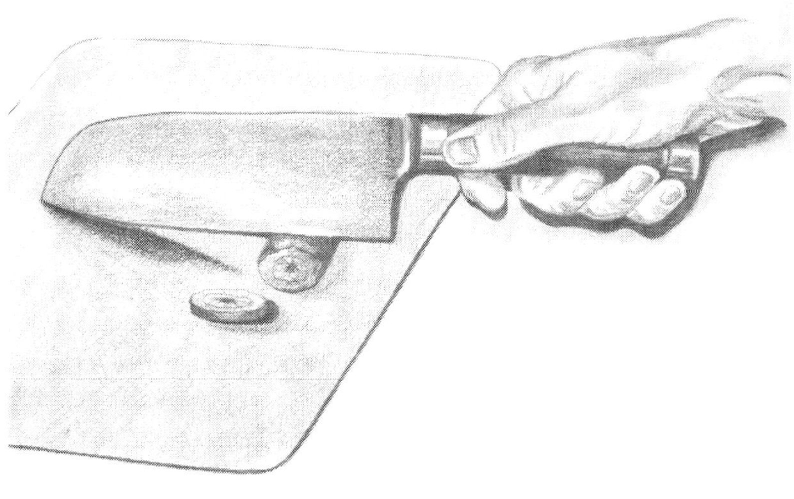

Using a large knife to chop vegetables

For general chopping and slicing, it is useful to have a 'cooks knife' with a slightly curved blade 15cm to 20cm (6in to 8in) long. When a knife of this type is used correctly, the wider part of the blade cuts through the vegetables with an up and down rocking motion, while the pointed end of the blade remains in contact with the chopping board. A large knife like this is quicker and less tiring to use than a small knife.

A small knife with a sharp blade about 8cm / 3¼in long is ideal for trimming Brussels sprouts and scoring baking potatoes.

A large chopping board is essential when preparing vegetables. A plastic one will not blunt the knives and can be washed in very hot water without warping or cracking. To prevent a chopping board slipping, put it on a non-slip mat or a damp dish cloth.

Straining vegetables

An accident can easily happen when a large and heavy pan of vegetables is being strained. Apart from the physical effort of lifting the pan, there is a risk of someone getting burnt or scalded, or the pan slipping off the draining board and causing an injury.

The following method of straining a large pan of vegetables reduces the chance of an accident, and also directs the contents of the pan into the colander so nothing is lost down the sink.

Straining a large pan of vegetables

Start by putting a suitable sized colander into the empty sink. Fold a damp dish cloth and put it on the draining board near the sink. Position the pan on the draining board, so it overlaps part of the cloth. The two pan handles should be facing towards and away from the sink. Lift off the pan lid, raising it first on the far side, so the steam escapes away from your face. Using an oven cloth, get hold of the handle furthest from the sink and carefully tip up the pan, so the water and vegetables fall into the colander.

The draining board will take the weight of the pan, while the damp cloth stops it slipping. A large wooden spoon or spatula can be used to remove any vegetable pieces that are clinging to the bottom of the pan.

Roast potatoes

Potatoes can be used whole or cut into pieces for roasting, depending on their size. Potatoes that have been cut tend to make crisper roasts. An acceptable weight for each prepared, uncooked roast potato (whole or cut piece) is about 75g / 2¾oz.

If you are offering another type of potato as well, allow between two and three roasts for each person, about 1.8kg / 4lb prepared weight for every 10 people.

If you are offering only roast potatoes, you may need to increase this to about 2.5kg / 5lb 10oz prepared weight for every 10 people.

It is usually easier for portion control if roast potatoes are counted rather than weighed. However, counting each potato as it is peeled can get very boring, and it is easy to make a mistake. Doing the potatoes in batches demands less concentration.

Start by making a note of how many potatoes are needed. Put some water in a large bowl, and as each potato is peeled, drop it in whole. When the bowl is full, take the potatoes out one by one, cut them into pieces as necessary, and transfer them into the saucepan, counting as you go. Keep a running total of how many potatoes (whole or cut pieces) are in the saucepan.

Keep potatoes covered with cold water so they do not turn black. Once prepared they can be left for several hours or even overnight, in a cool place.

To roast potatoes first parboil them and drain them. Brush some shallow tins with oil. Put a single layer of potatoes in each tin, and brush them with oil. If possible, roast them in a fairly hot oven. As they start to go brown, turn them over, so both sides get crisp. If they seem at all dry at this stage, brush them again with oil.

The potatoes will probably take between 1½ and 2½ hrs to roast, depending on the temperature of the oven and what else is being cooked at the same time. Large tins of potatoes take longer to roast than small ones.

A rectangular metal slotted server is a good utensil for dishing up roast potatoes.

Roast parsnips

Allow about 1kg / 2lb 4oz prepared weight of parsnips for every 10 people.

Parsnips do not need to be peeled, just top and tail and wash them. Cut each one into suitable sized pieces and cook them in a similar way to roast potatoes. Parsnips soon soften in boiling water, and they roast quicker than potatoes. They also tend to shrivel when roasted, and if the oven is very hot they are inclined to burn, so you have to keep an eye on them.

A rectangular metal slotted server is a good utensil for dishing up roast parsnips.

Mashed potatoes

If you are offering another type of potato as well, allow about 750g / 1lb 10oz prepared weight of potatoes for every 10 people. If you are offering only mashed potato, increase this to about 1.5kg / 3lb 6oz.

The potatoes can be prepared like roasts, but instead of counting them, weigh them and cut them into smaller pieces. Boil them until they are very soft, then drain them and return them to the pan. Mash them straight away, adding either margarine, butter and/or milk until they are creamy.

A catering sized potato masher is useful when mashing a large quantity of potatoes. A domestic masher is good for finishing off the mashing, and getting rid of any little lumps. If the potato is too deep in the pan to use a domestic masher, you may have to transfer it to a shallow bowl for a final mash.

Mashed potato can be kept hot for a while in the saucepan with a lid on. Do not have any heat under the pan. It can be dished up with a large spoon, or with a portioner (a gadget like an ice cream scoop). A portioner 5cm / 2in across (capacity 40ml / 1½fl oz) generously filled will give about 11 scoops from 750g / 1lb 10oz prepared weight of potatoes.

A small amount of horseradish sauce makes a tasty addition to mashed potato.

Baked potatoes

Baked potatoes are versatile and quick to prepare, and can be cooked at the same temperature as the other dishes in the oven. The cooking time depends on the size of the potatoes, the size of the baking trays, the heat of the oven, and how full the oven is. As a guide, at 200°C, 400°F, gas mark 6 a tray of potatoes that is sharing the oven with other dishes would probably take about 1½ hrs to cook. When there are a large number of potatoes filling a small oven, the steam they give off will tend to make their skins soft, rather than crisp.

Before baking them, score the potatoes or prick them all over with a fork, so the steam can escape. If they are scored around the middle, they are easy to cut in half once they are cooked. This is convenient for guests who like to put a knob of butter in their potato or share one potato with someone else. Put the larger potatoes round the edge of the baking tin and the smaller ones in the middle, to help them cook evenly. Halfway through the cooking time, turn the potatoes over so they brown on both sides.

If there is not the oven space to bake all the potatoes at once, they can be cooked ahead in batches, and then piled up in deeper trays to be reheated for the meal.

New potatoes

Small new potatoes that do not need peeling or cutting are quick to prepare, look attractive on the plate and are unlikely to fall apart.

If you are offering another type of potato as well, allow about 1.1kg / 2lb 8oz of new potatoes, prepared weight, for every 10 people.

(If they are being served in their skins, this will be unpeeled weight.) If you are offering only new potatoes, increase the weight to about 1.5kg / 3lb 6oz.

For a plated meal, it is often easier to base your calculations on the number of potatoes you are putting on each plate. Weigh a portion of potatoes, allowing for second helpings if necessary. Multiply that weight by the number of guests. Add a little more, especially if the potatoes vary considerably in size or quality.

If new potatoes are cooking too quickly and will be ready before they are needed, they can be slowed down by taking the pan off the heat for a short time. Once they are cooked and drained, new potatoes can be kept hot for a while if they are immediately returned to the saucepan and covered with a lid. Do not have any heat under the pan.

If you need to keep new potatoes hot for longer, they can be held in a colander over a pan of simmering water. Cover them with a large lid or foil, to keep the heat in.

New potatoes can be dished up with a large slotted spoon for plated meals, or a chip scoop for vegetable dishes.

Carrots

For large dinners, carrots are an ideal vegetable, being colourful, easy to cook and generally popular with guests. Allow about 700g / 1lb 8oz prepared weight for every 10 people.

If there are lots of carrots to prepare, it is much quicker to do them in batches, instead of one at a time:

Start by taking a double handful of carrots and put them on a chopping board. Peel them, top and tail them, then weigh them. Finally slice them, and tip them from the board into the pan. Then start again with another batch.

Although little batons look more elegant, it is quicker to cut carrots into rounds. They can be cut across two at a time if you put them side by side on the chopping board, and slice them across with a large knife.

Carrots can be slowed down whilst cooking, and kept hot in the same way as new potatoes. They can be dished up with a large slotted spoon for plated meals, or a chip scoop for vegetable dishes.

Peas and broad beans

Frozen peas and broad beans are easy vegetables for large scale catering. There is no preparation and the flavour is good. Allow about 700g / 1lb 8oz for every 10 people.

The easiest way to cook a large quantity of frozen peas or beans is to tip them into an empty pan, cover them with boiling water, and then bring them to the boil. Once the water gets to boiling point, they are nearly ready.

Peas and broad beans can be kept hot in a colander over simmering water, in the same way as new potatoes. They can be dished up with a large slotted spoon for plated meals, or a chip scoop for vegetable dishes.

Runner beans

Allow about 700g / 1lb 8oz of frozen or prepared fresh runner beans for every 10 people. Cooking a large quantity of frozen runner beans takes a long time, and they tend to lose their colour. They are generally more suitable for smaller dinners when it is easier to cook them quickly.

Brussels sprouts

Allow about 700g / 1lb 8oz prepared weight of sprouts for every 10 people.

If you are serving a plated meal, and the sprouts are a good size, you could base your calculations on how many sprouts you are putting on each plate. The method suggested for calculating the number of new potatoes is also suitable for sprouts *(page 72).*

It is tedious work preparing a large quantity of sprouts, but if you can sit down to do them, it is less tiring. For this method you need a small sharp knife, and three large bowls or containers, all within easy reach. One bowl is for unprepared sprouts, one for trimmings, and one for prepared sprouts.

Start by tipping the unprepared sprouts into one of the bowls. Taking one sprout at a time, hold it in your hand over one of the other bowls while you trim off any excess stalk and coarse outer leaves. Toss the finished sprout into the third bowl. Pick out another untrimmed sprout and start again.

There is no need to put down the knife during this process, neither do you need to cut a little cross in the base of each sprout – life is too short! Every so often, weigh the prepared sprouts and put them on one side for cooking later.

Sprouts should always be put into boiling water and cooked as quickly as possible to prevent them losing their colour and going soggy. Drain them well as soon as they are cooked. They can be kept hot for a short while in a colander over simmering water, in the same way as new potatoes. However, they will continue to cook while being held over the steam, and can fairly soon become soft and lose their colour.

If sprouts are cooking too quickly, and will be ready before they are needed, it is best to take action while they are still slightly firm. Strain them, and put them in a colander over simmering water, covered with a large lid or foil. They will continue to cook slowly in the steam. If they are not quite ready when it is time to dish up, tip them back into the simmering water for a few minutes to finish them off.

Sprouts can be dished up with a large slotted spoon for plated meals, or a chip scoop for vegetable dishes.

Broccoli

Allow about 650g / 1lb 6oz prepared weight of broccoli for every 10 people.

Broccoli florets are inclined to break up in boiling water, particularly when they have been cut. To help prevent this, it is better not to cut straight down through the florets, but instead, cut through some of the little branches that support them underneath, and then gently pull the florets apart.

To cook broccoli put the florets with their stems downwards into fairly shallow boiling water (maximum depth 15cm / 6in). If possible they should be in a single layer, not piled up in the water. They should be drained as soon as they are cooked.

If cooked broccoli florets are tipped from the pan into the colander, it must be done very gently or they will break up. Another way of straining broccoli is to pour some of the water out of the pan, then carefully lift out the florets using tongs, or a large slotted spoon, or by hand, wearing a pair of clean rubber gloves.

It is difficult to keep a large quantity of cooked broccoli hot, without it falling apart or losing its colour. It needs gentle handling while dishing up or the florets will break up.

Cauliflower

Allow about 650g / 1lb 6oz prepared weight of cauliflower for every 10 people.

Cook and drain cauliflower in a similar way to broccoli. It is a little more robust than broccoli and can be kept hot for a short while in a colander over simmering water, covered with a large lid or foil.

Cauliflower can also be kept hot in the oven as 'cauliflower cheese'. Place the cooked, drained cauliflower in a shallow dish and coat it with white sauce topped with grated cheese. For every 1kg / 2lb 4oz of prepared cauliflower, you need about 550ml / 1pt of white sauce and 100g / 3½oz grated cheese. This is a delicious way of serving cauliflower. If it is more convenient, the cauliflower can be cooked a short while ahead, coated in sauce and reheated during the first course.

Spring greens and cabbage

Allow about 500g / 1lb 2oz prepared weight of spring greens or cabbage for every 10 people.

Most varieties of greens are bulky to cook, so you need some big pans. Cut or tear any large leaves into pieces before cooking, this makes serving easier. Bring the water to the boil and push the greens down into it with a large wooden spoon. Once they are cooked, both spring greens and cabbage need thorough straining to get rid of excess water.

They can be kept hot for a short while in a colander over simmering water, covered with a large lid or foil. Tongs are a good utensil for dishing up spring greens and cabbage.

Red cabbage

Red cabbage mixed with onion and cooked in orange squash is delicious, especially with pork dishes. Use one medium sized onion for every 10 people. Weigh the peeled onion and then add enough prepared cabbage to bring the total weight to about 700g / 1lb 8oz for every 10 people.

Cover the bottom of a saucepan with about 2cm / ¾in of diluted orange squash that is a little stronger than usual, to give a good flavour. (Fresh orange juice can be used instead of orange squash, but add about 3 teaspoons of sugar for every 10 people.)

Shred the cabbage and finely chop the onion. Add them to the pan. Cover it and cook gently, stirring occasionally, until the cabbage is soft but not mushy. This might take up to an hour for a large quantity.

Red cabbage cooked in this way can be left in the pan until needed. If necessary, heat it through before service and then strain off the liquid. Red cabbage can be dished up with a large slotted spoon for plated meals, or a chip scoop for vegetable dishes.

Turnip and swede

These vegetables have a pleasant flavour if cooked in a little water with butter and seasoning. Allow about 700g / 1lb 8oz of prepared weight of turnip or swede for every 10 people.

Peel and dice the turnip or swede and put it in a pan with enough water to half cover it. For every 450g / 1lb prepared weight, add about 25g / 1oz of butter. Season with salt and pepper. Cover the pan and cook gently, stirring frequently until the turnip or swede is soft.

Once cooked, turnip and swede can be kept hot in their cooking liquid over a very low heat, providing you stir them from time to time so they do not stick to the bottom of the pan. Strain them before serving and dish them up with a slotted spoon for plated meals, or a chip scoop for vegetable dishes.

Turnip and swede can also be served mashed, in a similar way to potatoes.

Rice

If rice is being served as an accompaniment to a meat or fish dish, allow about 750g / 1lb 10oz for every 10 people.

Cook according to the instructions on the packet. Drain the cooked rice in a colander, and if necessary, run boiling water through it to separate the grains. Because of the risk of food poisoning, rice should be eaten as soon as possible after cooking. If it has to be kept hot for a short while, place the colander of cooked rice over simmering water. Cover it with a large lid or foil to keep the heat in.

If rice is to be served cold, as part of a salad, cool it quickly by running cold water through it while it is draining in a colander. It should then be kept under refrigeration and used within 24 hrs.

Vegetables au gratin

Vegetables baked in the oven under a crispy cheese or breadcrumb topping are delicious. Both the following recipes are very adaptable and can be cooked at different temperatures to fit in with other dishes in the oven. Once cooked, they can also be kept hot for a while without spoiling. They are best served in vegetable dishes, and less suited to a plated meal.

Layered potatoes and leeks

For easier portion control this recipe should be made in tins or dishes that are between 4cm and 5cm (1½in and 2in) deep.

Serves about 30.

2.7kg / 6lb peeled and thinly sliced potatoes
700g / 1lb 8oz chopped leeks
550ml / 1pt whole milk
500g / 1lb 2oz grated cheddar

Method
Grease the tin or dish.
Put half the sliced potatoes in the bottom and cover with the leeks.
Put the rest of the potatoes on top of the leeks.
Pour the milk evenly over the potatoes.
Cover the dish with foil and bake in a moderate oven 190°C, 375°F, gas mark 5 for about 45 min.
Remove the foil and spread the grated cheese over the top of the potatoes.
Return to the oven for about 45 min to finish cooking.
The dish is ready when the potatoes and leeks are soft and the cheese golden brown.

Parsnip and tomato bake

For easier portion control this recipe should be made in tins or dishes that are between 4cm and 5cm (1½in and 2in) deep.

Serves about 25.

2kg / 4lb 8oz thinly sliced parsnips
900g / 2lb sliced tomatoes
550ml / 1pt whole milk
450g / 1lb grated cheddar
225g / 8oz soft white breadcrumbs
salt and pepper

Method
Grease the tin or dish.
Put half the sliced parsnips in the bottom and cover with the sliced tomatoes.
Sprinkle with salt and pepper.
Put the rest of the parsnips on top of the tomatoes.
Pour the milk evenly over the parsnips.
Mix the breadcrumbs and cheese together and spread over the top.
Cover the dish with foil and bake in a moderate oven 190°C, 375°F, gas mark 5 for about 1½ hrs or until the parsnips are cooked.

Check the dish from time to time, and once the parsnips begin to soften, remove the foil, so the top can brown during the remainder of the cooking time.
The dish is ready when the parsnips are soft and the topping golden brown.

Salads

Some sections of Cold starters and hors d'oeuvres, page 39, are also relevant to salads.

Because there is very little cooking involved, a salad is usually easier than a hot meal. The cooker is hardly used, so there is plenty of room for soup on top and perhaps hot puddings inside. For people who are not used to serving at table, plates of salad are easy to carry. Also, if the service of the meal is rather slow, at least the guests are not watching their food go cold.

However, assembling a large number of plated salads can take quite a while and the finished plates use up a lot of space. Because they include high risk food items, like cold meat, fish or egg, plated salads should be kept under refrigeration until shortly before service. This can be a problem unless you have a very large refrigerator. One way round this difficulty is to plate up the salad vegetables earlier, and add the high risk food just before service.

Salad vegetables – how much to buy?

Not many salad vegetables are sold by weight, making it difficult to work out how much to buy for a large dinner. The following guide may be helpful:

Lettuce – An iceberg lettuce usually weighs about 450g / 1lb. A round lettuce usually weighs about 225g / 8oz.

Tomatoes – Most varieties of tomato weigh between 50g and 85g (2oz and 3oz). A cherry tomato weighs between 10g and 15g (about ½oz).

Cucumber – Every 2.5cm / 1in of cucumber (not including the narrow ends) will give about 8 thin slices.

Cress – A tub of cress will garnish about 8 plated salads.

Beetroot – A thin slice from a small cooked beetroot weighs between 10g and 15g (about ½oz).

Radishes – A radish without leaves weighs about 10g / ½oz.

Spring onions – A spring onion, including some of the green stalk, weighs about 10g / ½oz.

Main items in a salad – approximate quantities for 10 people

Quiche and pork pie – 1.5kg / 3lb 6oz
Shelled prawns – 1kg / 2lb 4oz
Fresh salmon – 1.2kg / 2lb 11oz uncooked weight
Tinned tuna and salmon – 800g / 1lb 12oz
Cooked beef, turkey and ham – 800g / 1lb 12oz

If you are cooking the meat yourself to serve cold, the suggested quantities for roast meat on pages 56, 57 and 58 will provide a generous portion.

Additional items in a salad

The salad garnish that is suggested for hors d'oeuvres on page 42 can also be used in a plated salad. To make it more substantial, add some extra lettuce and one or two additional items, for example:

Hard boiled eggs, sliced or quartered
Stuffed eggs
Cottage or grated cheese
Coleslaw
Sweetcorn kernels
Chopped celery
Radishes
Sliced beetroot (add it shortly before service or it may discolour the salad)
Spring onions
Grated carrot

Green salad served in bowls

Instead of serving the salad as a fully plated meal, the salad vegetables and potatoes can be served in dishes or bowls for people to help themselves.

Green salad for about 5 people

100g / 3½oz lettuce
¼ cucumber
170g / 6oz tomatoes
5 or 6 radishes
½ stick of celery
sprinkling of cress (for garnishing the salad)
5 spring onions and ½ a pepper (optional)*

Green salad for about 30 people

600g / 1lb 5oz lettuce (different varieties give added interest and colour to the salad)
1½ cucumbers
1kg / 2lb 4oz tomatoes
350g / 12oz radishes
3 sticks of celery
1 tub of cress (for garnishing the salads)
300g / 10½oz spring onions and 3 peppers (optional)*

Green salad for about 50 people

1kg / 2lb 4oz lettuce (different varieties give added interest and colour to the salad)
2 long cucumbers or 2½ short ones
1.75kg / 3lb 15oz tomatoes
550g / 1lb 4oz radishes
5 sticks of celery
2 tubs of cress (for garnishing the salads)
500g / 1lb 2oz spring onions and 5 peppers (optional)*

*Some people find spring onions and peppers indigestible. If adding them to the salad, it is best to leave them in easily recognisable pieces.

Tomatoes

If you are using sliced tomatoes in the salad, it is usually better to put them in a separate dish, particularly if they are very ripe. When there are a number of people helping themselves from a large bowl of salad, the pieces of tomato can easily break up and fall apart. Little cherry tomatoes left whole are a good choice if you want to put the tomatoes in the salad bowl.

Potatoes

Baked or new potatoes go well with salad. Because a salad is usually a lighter meal, people tend to eat more potatoes than they would with a hot meal.

Allow about 1.8kg / 4lb of new potatoes for every 10 people. If it is a plated meal, the section on new potatoes on page 72, gives another method of calculating the quantity of potatoes you need to buy.

If you cannot serve baked or new potatoes, then potato salad is a good alternative.

Potato salad

Serves about 30. If you are also offering baked or new potatoes, this quantity will serve up to 50.

3.6kg / 8lb new or salad potatoes
Either 500ml / 18fl oz salad cream
or 500ml / 18fl oz of a mixture of mayonnaise and vinaigrette

Method
Boil the potatoes until just cooked, drain and cut into pieces.
While still warm stir in the salad cream, or mayonnaise mixed with vinaigrette.

Chives or the green part of spring onions, finely chopped and either stirred into the salad, or sprinkled on top, give added flavour and an attractive contrast of colour.

The following recipes are useful if you want to offer a selection of salads. They can all be prepared several hours in advance and stored in covered containers in a refrigerator.

Rice salad

Serves about 25.

450g / 1lb long grain rice (white or wholegrain)
350g / 12oz frozen peas
350g / 12oz sweetcorn kernels (tinned or frozen)
2 red or green peppers
350g / 12oz mushrooms
Vegetable stock

Method
Cook the rice, drain it in a colander, and cool it quickly by running cold water through it as it drains.
Cook the peas and sweetcorn and drain them well.
Halve and core the peppers and place in boiling water for 30 seconds, cool them under cold water, drain and chop.
Chop the mushrooms, cook in a little stock until they begin to soften, drain well.
Mix all the ingredients together in a bowl.

Coleslaw

Serves about 40.

1.1kg / 2lb 8oz hard white cabbage
500g / 1lb 2oz carrots
180g / 6½oz onion
600g / 1lb 5oz either mayonnaise or salad cream

Method
Finely chop or grate the cabbage.
Grate the carrot and onion.
Mix them well, and stir in the mayonnaise or salad cream.

For a sharper, less creamy coleslaw, replace half the mayonnaise or salad cream with vinaigrette.

Sausage and bean salad

Serves about 40.

1kg / 2lb 4oz cooked smoked sausage
500g / 1lb 2oz cauliflower
600g / 1lb 5oz broad beans (fresh or frozen)
600g / 1lb 5oz tinned red kidney beans (drained weight)
600g / 1lb 5oz tinned butter beans (drained weight)
1 large red onion
280ml / ½ pt vinaigrette mixed with 120g / 4oz mayonnaise

Method
Cook the broad beans.
Slice or chop the sausage.
Divide the cauliflower into very small florets.
Slice the onion thinly across and separate into rings.
Rinse the red kidney beans and butter beans and drain well.
Mix all the ingredients together and stir in the vinaigrette and mayonnaise.

Hot puddings

Hot puddings are very popular, but can be difficult to make when catering for large numbers. If you are busy with the main course, there is often neither the time to make a pudding, nor any room in the oven to cook it. Because of this, it is usually easier to choose a pudding that can be cooked ahead and reheated nearer the time.

Because they are portioned and dished up straight from the oven, hot puddings tend to be slower to serve than cold desserts. Also, depending on the kitchen, it can sometimes be difficult to warm the pudding bowls.

On the positive side, hot puddings stay in the oven and out of the way until you want them, leaving the kitchen work surface and refrigerator free for other things.

Flans, tarts and fruit pies

Flans, tarts and fruit pies are all suitable for a large dinner if they are made in domestic sized dishes or tins that will serve up to about eight people. They are not such a good choice if you are using larger square or rectangular dishes or tins. If flans and tarts are made in these larger dishes, the portions from the middle will not have a pastry edge, and look different from the others. If a fruit pie is made in a large dish, the pastry is inclined to shrink away around the edges, and become moist and heavy in the middle.

When the pudding is going to be made in a large dish or tin, a baked sponge or fruit crumble is a good choice.

Portion control and dishing up

Most flans, tarts, fruit pies, sponge puddings and crumbles can be portioned in a similar way to meat pies *(page 62)*.

It saves time if the pudding bowls are counted out in advance. When it is time to serve the pudding, divide the bowls into several similar sized piles and put them in a convenient spot for dishing up, and from where the waiters can easily reach them.

Portion the first pudding and dish it up into the bowls on the top of each pile. As the waiters take the filled bowls, continue dishing up into the empty ones underneath. Everyone has to work fast, as once the puddings leave the oven they soon cool down.

Custard

As a guide, 550ml / 1pt of custard will serve about 6 people. For every 10 people allow about 900ml / just over 1½pt of custard.

If you need to make a large quantity of custard, the instantvariety in packets is an easy option, especially if you can spare a large saucepan to make it in. Measure out the water, bring it to the boil and then whisk in the instant powder.

The custard can be made before the meal and heated up for serving. Once it is made, putting a lid on the pan will help to prevent a skin forming. Custard can be dished up in a similar way to gravy *(page 59)*.

Of course, instant custard can also be made during the meal in a measuring jug, following the instructions on the packet. This is less convenient when you are catering for a large number of people as you can only make a few portions at a time, and have to keep making more custard while you are busy dishing up the puddings.

Depending upon the choice of pudding, it is likely that one or two people will not want custard, or request pouring cream instead. Occasionally someone might ask for a bowl of custard instead of a pudding.

Baked sponge pudding

This is an easy pudding to make, and if the oven is crowded, you can start it off on a lower shelf and move it up later as space permits. A baked sponge can also be made several hours before it is needed and then reheated. Covering the pudding with foil when reheating it, will help to keep it moist.

Upside down sponge pudding

It can be difficult to turn out a large upside down sponge pudding without it sticking or breaking. To make it easier, prepare the dish or tin before putting in the raw pudding mixture. First grease the sides and bottom with butter or margarine. Then cover the bottom with greaseproof paper, and grease the paper with butter or margarine.

When the pudding is taken from the oven, leave it to rest for a few minutes, then run a knife around the edges. Cover the pudding with a large chopping board or tray and carefully turn it over. Once the pudding has slipped out of its dish onto the board or tray, the greaseproof paper can be peeled off and the pudding served.

If you are making an upside down sponge pudding to reheat later, carefully slide the pudding off the board or tray and back into the tin it was cooked in, but the right way up for serving. To prevent the greaseproof paper sticking, peel if off while the pudding is still warm. Cover the pudding with foil to prevent it drying out while it is being reheated.

Fruit crumbles

A fruit crumble is a good choice if the pudding is going to be made in a large dish or tin where some of the portions will be taken from the middle. It is a quick and easy pudding to make, and if the oven is crowded, you can start it off on a lower shelf and move it up later as space permits.

If it is made in a large dish or tin, the crumble topping in the middle may take longer to brown than the crumble around the edges. Covering the edges with foil will give the middle a chance to catch up.

A crumble can be made several hours before it is needed and then reheated.

Plain sponge

This plain sponge can be easily added to and adapted to give a variety of hot puddings. The quantities in this recipe will serve about 30 depending on what other ingredients are in the pudding.

900g / 2lb caster sugar
900g / 2lb self-raising flour
900g / 2lb margarine
15 beaten eggs (medium size)
125ml / 4fl oz milk

Method

Cream together the margarine and sugar.
Gradually add the eggs and flour, mixing well.
Stir in the milk.
Spoon the mixture into the dishes or tins, spreading it evenly to the edges.
Bake at 180°C, 350°F, gas mark 4 for about 1 hr, depending on the size of the dishes.

When cooked, the sponge should feel springy to the touch, and a knife blade pushed into it should come out clean.

Apple and lemon sponge

This is a pudding with a delicious moist tang that can be made in pie dishes, casserole dishes or even heavy roasting tins.

Serves about 30.

Plain sponge recipe x 1, see above
1.5kg / 3lb 6oz peeled and cored cooking apples
800g / 1lb 12oz lemon curd (approx)

Method

Slice the apples.
Make up the plain sponge recipe.
Cover the bottom of the dishes with a layer of sliced apple.
Drop teaspoons of lemon curd evenly over the apple pieces.
Cover the apple and lemon curd with the sponge mixture.
Bake as for the plain sponge recipe.

Notes on the recipe

It does not matter if a little more or less lemon curd is used than suggested in the recipe, but it should have a good flavour. If the apples are put into cold water as they are peeled, they will not turn brown.

Pineapple upside down sponge

This pudding is always popular, and as each portion includes one whole pineapple ring, it is very easy to portion and dish up. For notes on upside down sponge puddings see page 84.

Serves 30.

Plain sponge recipe x 1*(page 85)* using demerara sugar instead of caster sugar
40 tinned pineapple rings (either in syrup or juice)
30 glacé cherries

Syrup topping
100g / 3½oz butter
85g / 3oz golden syrup
70g / 2½oz demerara sugar
40ml / 1½fl oz water

Method
Prepare each baking dish.
Drain the pineapple rings and place 30 of them side by side to cover the base of each dish.
Cut the cherries in half, and place one half, cut side up, in the centre of each pineapple ring.
Chop the remaining cherries and left over pieces of pineapple.
Use them to fill in the gaps between the pineapple rings, and scatter any extra pieces over the top.
Make up the plain sponge recipe.
Cover the pineapple and cherries with the sponge mixture.
Bake as for the plain sponge.
After peeling off the greaseproof paper, brush the pudding with syrup topping.

Making syrup topping
Using a small heavy pan, gently warm all the ingredients until the butter has melted and the sugar dissolved.
Boil for one minute.
Leave for a few seconds until the bubbles subside, then brush it over the sponge.

Notes on the recipe
If the pudding is made ahead to reheat later, do not add the syrup topping until just before service.

A tinned pineapple ring will weigh about 35g.
There are about 20 glacé cherries in 1 x 100g tub.

Cherry and walnut upside down sponge

Those who like cherries and walnuts will love this rather extravagant sponge pudding, which is delicious served with pouring cream. For notes on upside down sponge puddings see page 84.

Serves about 30.

Plain sponge recipe x 1*(page 85)*
300g / 10½oz butter
300g / 10½oz soft brown sugar
40g / 1½oz instant coffee powder or granules
140ml / ¼pt boiling water
425g / 15oz roughly chopped glacé cherries
425g / 15oz walnut pieces

Method
Prepare each baking dish.
Melt the butter in a saucepan then add the sugar, instant coffee and boiling water.
Stir well over a low heat to dissolve the sugar.
Add the cherries and walnuts.
Spread the mixture evenly over the base of each dish.
Make up the plain sponge recipe.
Cover the cherries and walnuts with the sponge mixture.
Bake as for the plain sponge.

Jam upside down sponge

This is an economical pudding that is quick to prepare and always popular. For notes on upside down sponge puddings see page 84.

Serves about 30.

Plain sponge recipe x 1 *(page 85)*
1.5kg / 3lb 6oz good quality jam

Method
Prepare each baking dish.
Spread the jam evenly over the base of each dish. (If the jam is too thick to spread easily, soften it in a small pan over a low heat.)
Make up the plain sponge recipe.
Cover the jam with the sponge mixture.
Bake as for the plain sponge, being careful to keep the base of the dishes away from a heat source while the pudding is cooking, or the jam might burn round the edges.

Crumble topping

Serves about 30 with a fairly thick layer of crumble.

1.2kg / 2lb 11oz flour (plain or self-raising)
600g / 1lb 5oz margarine
600g / 1lb 5oz caster sugar

Method
Rub the fat into the flour and stir in the caster sugar.
Sprinkle the mixture over the fruit, pressing it down gently.
Smooth the top of the crumble.

Notes on the recipe
Crumble topping can be prepared several days ahead and left in a covered container in the refrigerator. It can also be made ahead and frozen.
If using bought crumble topping you need about 2.4kg / 5lb 4oz for 30 portions.
For a crumble topping with a difference – replace some of the white flour with wholemeal flour or porridge oats.

Apple crumble

Serves about 30.

Crumble topping x 1, see above
3.1kg / 7lb peeled and cored cooking apples
250g / 9oz caster sugar
425ml / ¾pt water

Method
Cut the apples into slices and put them in the bottom of each dish or tin.
Pour over the water and sprinkle with the caster sugar.
Cover with crumble topping and cook at 190°C, 375°F, gas mark 5 for about 40 min or until the fruit is soft and the crumble golden brown.
Lower the temperature if the crumble is coloured but the fruit is not quite cooked.

Notes on the recipe
If the apples are put in cold water as they are peeled, they will not turn brown.
For apple and blackberry crumble, replace some of the apple slices with the same weight of blackberries.

This recipe can be easily converted to a quickly made peach or apricot crumble. Use the same weight of drained, tinned fruit but do not add any water or caster sugar.

Meringue topped baked apples

This recipe is an interesting alternative to traditional baked apples and can be served with custard, pouring cream or ice cream.

Serves 20.

10 whole cooking apples – about 275g / 9½oz each
280g / 10oz raisins, currants or sultanas (or a mixture)

8 egg whites
450g / 1lb caster sugar

Method

Core the apples and halve them by cutting across.
Put them in a shallow pan of simmering water (the water should come half way up the apple halves).
Cook for 5 min then turn them over and cook them for another 5 min.
Drain them and put them cut side up in a dish or tin, with a space of at least 2.5cm / 1in between them.
Fill them with the dried fruit.

Whip the egg whites until very stiff.
Gradually whisk in the sugar.
Either pipe or spoon the meringue mixture over the top of the apple halves.
Cook at about 170°C, 325°F, gas mark 3 for about 20 min or until the meringue is starting to colour.

Notes on the recipe

The apples can be cooked and filled several hours ahead, and left in their dishes ready for the meringue topping. Once cooked, this dish can be held for a while at a lower temperature, but not for long or the meringue may start to collapse.
Be careful dishing up – if the apples are tipped sideways the meringue topping can easily slide off!

Leftover egg yolks can be frozen to use later. To prevent them becoming thick and 'gummy' first whisk them up with caster sugar using 15g / ½oz of sugar for every 6 yolks.
6 yolks, with 280ml / ½pt of milk and another 15g / ½oz of caster sugar, will make about three portions of rich egg custard.

Sometimes a recipe may result in leftover egg whites, instead of yolks. If you want to make meringue from leftover egg whites but do not know how many there are, weigh them and use about 1¾ of their weight in caster sugar.

Cold desserts

When catering for a large dinner, a cold dessert is usually easier than a hot pudding, and there are plenty of recipes to choose from. The ideal dessert is one that looks attractive, can be prepared ahead, and not need much last minute attention. It should also be quick to dish up with everyone's portion looking the same.

Some desserts are suitable for a buffet, but not for a sit-down meal. For example, a beautifully decorated trifle would look splendid on a buffet table, but at a sit-down meal, the guests would be unlikely to see it at its best. They would only see their own portion – a creamy mix of sponge and fruit!

Ice cream desserts

Ice cream desserts that come straight from freezer to table are invaluable if time is short. A dessert based around ice cream and fruit that can be prepared whilst people are eating their main course can also be useful on occasions.

Pouring cream

People vary in the amount of cream they take. As a guide 280ml / ½pt of cream will serve about 10 people if it is a creamy dessert, a mousse or fresh fruit salad. For other desserts, especially flans and pies, allow nearly twice as much. If possible serve the cream in small jugs so people can help themselves.

Profiteroles with chocolate sauce

These are always popular and suitable for any occasion. They can be made the day before and stored in a covered container. Profiteroles also freeze well, with or without the cream filling.

Serves about 20 (3 profiteroles each).

275g / 9½oz plain flour
225g / 8oz butter
1 heaped teaspoon caster sugar
550ml / 1pt water
7/8 beaten eggs*
700ml / 1¼pt double or whipping cream (approx)

***For accuracy, weigh the whole eggs in their shells before you start. The total weight should be about 425g / 15oz.**

Chocolate sauce (makes about 700ml / 1¼ pt)
450g / 1lb plain chocolate broken into pieces
120g / 4oz golden syrup
140ml / ¼pt milk
70g / 2½oz butter
25g / 1oz instant coffee, dissolved in 30ml / 2 tablespoons of hot water

Method

Sieve the flour and leave on one side.
Put the water, sugar and butter in a saucepan.
Heat gently to melt the butter and then bring to the boil.
Immediately remove from the heat and add the flour, mixing well until smooth.
The mixture should form a soft mass, and start to leave the sides of the pan. (If this does not happen, put the pan on a low heat for a few seconds, stirring well.)
Leave to cool for about 10 min.

Gradually add the eggs, beating well, until the mixture is smooth and shiny, and firm enough to stand in soft peaks when lifted with a spoon.
Using a piping bag and plain nozzle, between 1cm and 2cm (½in and ¾in) wide, pipe 60 to 75 little mounds onto greased baking trays.
Bake at 200°C, 400°F, gas mark 6 for about 25 min until well puffed, golden coloured and firm.
Cool on a wire rack.

Whip the cream. Split open the profiteroles and fill with whipped cream.

Pour over the warm chocolate sauce just before serving.

To make the chocolate sauce on a hob:

Put all the ingredients in a bowl.
Put the bowl over a pan of simmering water, stirring from time to time, until the sauce is smooth and glossy. If it is too thick, stir in more milk.

Make sure the bottom of the bowl does not touch the water or you may have fudge instead of sauce! A sieve or colander placed across the top of the pan makes a good support for a small bowl.

To make the chocolate sauce in the microwave:

Put all the ingredients in a microwave jug or bowl.
Microwave on full power for 1 min, stir well.
If the chocolate has not melted, microwave it again for 10 seconds, and stir.
Repeat as necessary until the sauce is smooth and glossy. If it is too thick, stir in more milk.

Notes on the recipe

To split open the profiteroles, use a small pair of pointed scissors, making one single cut half way across each little puff. Piping the cream into the profiteroles is quicker and less messy than using a spoon. You can use the same nozzle as you used for making the profiteroles.
The chocolate sauce can be made ahead and kept in a refrigerator for several days, and reheated either in the microwave or over hot water. As it cools down, the sauce will thicken slightly and eventually become difficult to pour, so you need to work quickly. If you are serving a large number of people, it is best to keep the sauce warm, (but not on direct heat) and decant it as needed into a smaller jug for pouring over the profiteroles. A jug is quicker and less messy than a ladle.
If you are making a different type of sauce, also allow about 700ml / 1¼pt for 20 servings.

Individual sherry trifles

Individual trifles, served in pretty glass dishes, look most attractive on the table, and are a very popular dessert.

For 10 servings (using dishes approx 140ml / 5fl oz capacity).

250g / 9oz of jam Swiss roll or sponge cake
100ml / 3½fl oz sweet sherry
400g / 14oz tinned fruit cocktail in syrup or juice (drained weight)
140ml / ¼pt of liquid jelly (orange, strawberry or raspberry)
500ml / 18fl oz thick custard
425ml / ¾pt double or whipping cream
5 glacé cherries
decorations

Method

Leave the custard to cool, stirring occasionally to prevent a skin forming.
Leave the jelly to cool but do not allow it to set.

Put a slice of Swiss roll or sponge cake in the bottom of each dish.
Pour over 10ml / 2 teaspoons of sherry.
Drain the fruit cocktail and divide it between the dishes.
Pour over 15ml / 1 tablespoon of liquid jelly.
Leave it at least 30 min, then spoon in the custard, dividing it between the dishes.
Leave the trifles to cool.

Whip the cream stiffly and either spread it over the custard, or pipe it using a large star nozzle.
Place half a glacé cherry in the centre of each trifle, and decorate.

Notes on the recipe

Most of the preparation can be done ahead, adding the cream and decorations nearer the time. Suitable decorations include coloured sugar strands, angelica, chocolate flakes and toasted almonds. Coloured sugar strands should not be sprinkled on the trifles until the last minute, or the colours will run into the cream.

Raspberries or strawberries can be used instead of fruit cocktail, and the top of the trifle decorated with small pieces of the same fruit.

The most efficient way of making the trifles is to lay out all the empty dishes, and then do one stage of the recipe at once, across them all, before moving onto the next stage.
The quickest way to portion out the jelly and sherry is to use a small jug, and pour it from there into a measuring spoon, held just above each trifle. If you have some liquid jelly left over, it is better not to add it to the trifles, as it could make them too sweet. (The same advice does not apply to the sherry!)

A large trifle looks more attractive on the buffet table if it fills most of the bowl or serving dish, rather than coming only half way up the sides. Also, if the trifle is not much deeper than 6cm / 2½in, it is easier to make sure each serving includes some sponge and fruit, as well as custard and cream. If you are using the previous recipe, it is not difficult to check if your bowl is likely to be a suitable size for the trifle. Firstly multiply a single serving of about 140ml / 5fl oz by the number of portions you plan to make. Measure out this amount of water and pour it into the bowl or serving dish. The water level will give you an idea of the size of the trifle.
There are about 20 glacé cherries in 1 x 100g tub.

Fresh fruit salad

Fresh fruit salad makes a refreshing light dessert after a heavy meal, and although time-consuming to prepare, most of it can be done several hours ahead.

For 10 servings allow approx 1.35kg / 3lb of prepared fruit.

Making fruit salad

For a fruit salad to look and taste delicious, it needs a good variety of fruit. Producing a large quantity of fruit salad is a time consuming job, but it can be done several hours ahead, though not the day before, or some of the fruit will begin to deteriorate.

Choose a bowl that is large enough to hold all the prepared fruit, and pour in some fruit juice. Orange, apple and pineapple are all suitable and a mixture of juice gives an interesting flavour. Adding a dash of orange squash to the juice will give it a pleasant hint of sweetness.

Before preparing any fruit, work out the total weight of fruit salad you need to make, and write it down. As each variety of fruit is prepared, make a note of its weight before putting it in the bowl. Keep a running total of the weight of the prepared fruit.

As more fruit is added to the bowl, the juice will need topping up. It should just cover the fruit to prevent any sliced apples or pears from discolouring. As a guide, for every 30 portions of fruit salad you will need about 1ltr / 1¾pt of juice.

Apart from bananas, any fruit that is going to be added later can be prepared along with the rest, weighed and put in a separate container until needed. The weight of this extra fruit should be added to the running total of prepared fruit. With bananas, it is best to estimate their prepared weight *(page 141)*.

When the total weight has been reached, give the fruit a good stir and put the bowl in the refrigerator. If there is not enough space, covering the bowl with cold wet tea towels will help to keep it cool.

Preparing the fruit

Apples – use apples with different coloured skins, and cut them into pieces without peeling them. The cut pieces must be quickly stirred into the juice or they will start to turn brown.

Apricots, greengages – slice without peeling.

Bananas – bananas are usually sliced into rounds, but it is better not to prepare them until a short time before service, as they soon become soft and discoloured.

Cherries – the preparation is quicker and neater with a cherry stoner, and the cherries can be added whole. If they are dark and juicy, it is better to add them shortly before service, in case the colour runs into the other fruit.

Grapes – cut in half and remove any seeds. Small seedless grapes can be used whole.

Kiwi fruit – peel and cut into thick chunks so they do not break up, or slice into rounds and use as part of the garnish.

Melons – if possible use different types for a variation in colour and flavour. Make melon balls from the flesh, or cut it into chunks.

Oranges, satsumas, tangerines – cut or break into segments, being careful to remove any pips.

Peaches, nectarines – they are usually peeled and then sliced.

Pears – they should be ripe but not soft, and are usually peeled before slicing. The cut pieces must be quickly stirred into the juice or they will start to turn brown.

Pineapple – remove skin and core, and cut into neat pieces.

Plums – cut them into pieces. Dark plums should not be added to the fruit salad until shortly before service, as the colour will run into the other fruit.

Raspberries – usually placed on top or at the side of the fruit salad as part of the garnish.

Strawberries – small fruits can be left whole, larger ones halved or sliced. They are often used as part of the garnish.

Using tinned fruit

If time is short and you need to make some extra fruit salad, tinned fruit, preferably in its own juice, can be very useful. Suitable tinned fruit includes pineapple, peaches, kiwi fruit, pears and apricots. Tinned fruit cocktail, without the brightly coloured cherries, makes a good base for a fruit salad

Dishing up fruit salad If there is space, lay out all the empty plates or bowls and divide the fruit salad between them. Then add some extra juice to any that need it, and check that each portion looks similar. A simple decoration, for example, half a strawberry and a slice of kiwi fruit, can now be added.

Notes on the recipe
Fruit salad that is more than a day old starts to deteriorate in appearance. To refresh leftover fruit salad, put it in a large sieve and strain off and discard the juice. Run cold water through the fruit, and pick out any pieces of fruit which have discoloured or gone soft. Then put the fruit salad in a container, and pour over some more fruit juice.
Fruit salad can be converted into a 'tropical fruit chow chow' by replacing the apples and pears with more exotic ingredients like mangoes, water chestnuts and lychees. If these are tinned, add the juice to give extra flavour.

Banana split

This dessert is enjoyed by most people and is a useful standby when time is short.

Serves 24.

24 small to medium sized bananas
2 rectangular blocks of vanilla ice cream each 1ltr*
600ml / just over 1pt double or whipping cream
12 glacé cherries

Half the recipe for chocolate sauce on pages 90-91 (about 350ml / 12fl oz)

***The easiest ice cream to use is the long narrow 1ltr block which can be cut into slices.**

Method
Make the chocolate sauce and keep it warm.
Whip the cream.
Slice the bananas in half lengthways.
Cut each block of ice cream into 12 slices.
Put two slices of banana into each dish, with a slice of ice cream between them, pushing the cut sides of the banana against the ice cream.
Using a large star nozzle, pipe a zig zag of cream across the top of the ice cream and banana.
Drizzle some sauce over the top and decorate each dessert with half a cherry.

Notes on the recipe
The recipe can be varied by using a different flavoured ice cream, or by using caramel or melba sauce instead of chocolate. If using a bought sauce allow about 350ml / 12fl oz for this quantity.
This dessert requires very little advance preparation, especially if you buy the sauce rather than making it. When time is really short it can be made during the main course.
However, because it has to be assembled at the last minute, banana split takes a while to dish up, so is not really suitable for a large dinner.

Orange meringue surprise

This dessert is an interesting mix of sweet meringue and fresh orange. It is ideal if you are short of dishes or eating outside, as the orange skins are disposable! It should be served with small jugs of pouring cream.

Serves 10.

5 very large oranges (weighing about 300g / 10½oz each)
50g / 2oz cornflour
120g / 4oz caster sugar
850ml / 1½pt orange juice (from the flesh of the oranges and a carton)
4 egg yolks

6 egg whites
350g / 12oz caster sugar

Method

Using a thin, pointed knife, cut each orange round the middle in a zig zag line.
Separate the two halves, and if necessary cut a thin slice off the bottom of each so they sit firmly.

Remove the orange flesh and extract as much juice as possible. This can best be done with a juice extractor. Alternatively, put the orange flesh in a large sieve, and stand it over a bowl. Push the orange flesh down with a wooden spoon to squeeze out the juice.

Make up the volume of juice with some orange juice from a carton.
Stand the orange halves on baking tins, leaving at least 2.5cm / 1in between them.
Put the cornflour and the 120g / 4oz caster sugar in a bowl and gradually mix in enough juice to give a thin, smooth cream.
Bring the remaining juice to the boil and pour it onto the cornflour mixture, stirring well.
Return it to the pan and bring to the boil again, stirring constantly, until the sauce thickens and becomes smooth.
Remove from the heat and leave to cool for a few minutes.
Stir in the egg yolks.
Pour the mixture into the orange halves.

Whip the egg whites until very stiff.
Gradually whisk in the 350g / 12oz caster sugar.
Either pipe or spoon the meringue mixture over the orange halves.
Cook at about 170° C, 325°F, gas mark 3 for about 20 min or until the meringue is firm to the touch and golden brown.
Leave the meringue topped oranges to cool for a while before serving them.

Notes on the recipe

Although the preparation of the oranges takes a while, it can be done a day or two ahead, and the orange skins can be filled several hours before the meal. This just leaves the meringue topping to make nearer the time.
As a guide, the oranges should produce about half the orange juice needed for this recipe.

The following two desserts make use of bought sponge flan cases. These are readily available and very useful as a base for a cold dessert, especially when you are short of time or help in the kitchen.

Orange meringue sponge

This dish is similar to the previous recipe for orange meringue surprise, but uses a sponge flan case instead of fresh oranges.

A 220g sponge flan case 25cm / 10in across will give about 8 portions.

For each sponge flan allow:

500ml / 18fl oz orange juice (from oranges or a carton)
40g / 1½oz cornflour
70g / 2½oz caster sugar
3 egg yolks

5 egg whites
300g / 10½oz caster sugar

Method

Brush a large, flat ovenproof plate with plenty of melted butter to help prevent the flan from sticking.

Put the cornflour and the 70g / 2½oz caster sugar in a bowl and gradually mix in enough orange juice to give a thin, smooth cream.
Bring the remaining juice to the boil and pour it onto the cornflour mixture, stirring well.
Return it to the pan and bring to the boil again, stirring constantly, until the sauce thickens.
Remove from the heat and leave to cool for a few minutes.
Stir in the egg yolks.
Pour the mixture into the sponge flan case and leave to cool.

Whip the egg whites until very stiff.
Gradually whisk in the 300g / 10½oz caster sugar.
Either pipe or spoon the meringue mixture over the flan cases.
Cook at about 170°C, 325°F, gas mark 3 for about 20 min or until the meringue is firm to the touch and golden brown.
Serve warm or leave the flan to cool.

Notes on the recipe

If the meringue is first piped or spooned round the edges of the flan, before doing the middle, it is less likely to slide off the orange filling. For a suggested method of cutting a flan into an uneven number of portions see page 62.

Fruit sponge flan

This is a very useful dessert that can be made with tinned or fresh fruit, depending on the occasion, the time of year and your budget.

A 220g sponge flan case 25cm / 10in across will give about 8 portions.

For each sponge flan allow:

500g / 1lb 2oz of either fresh fruit, prepared weight
Or, tinned fruit (in syrup or juice) drained weight
and about 1½ x 35g sachets of Quick Jel.

Suitable fresh fruit includes: apricots, cherries, kiwi fruit, mandarins, peaches, pears, raspberries and strawberries.

Suitable tinned fruit includes: apricots, cherries, mandarins, peaches, pears and pineapple.

Method
Cut the fruit into even sized pieces and arrange it in the flans.
Cover it with Quick Jel according to the instructions.

Notes on the recipe
If using several different fruits, aim for an attractive contrast of colour. When the flans are cut, each portion should look similar. For a suggested method of cutting a flan into an uneven number of portions see page 62.
Quick Jel does as the name suggests, and once it begins to thicken it sets quite quickly. If there are several flans to glaze you have to work fast. If the Quick Jel begins to set before it has all been used, it can be re-warmed over a low heat.
To save time the flans can be glazed with apricot jam instead of Quick Jel. Allow about 80g of jam and 40ml of water for each flan. Bring the jam and water to the boil in a small pan, stirring well. Sieve the mixture and cool it a little before brushing over the fruit.
A fruit flan looks attractive decorated with generous swirls of whipped cream topped with small pieces of fruit. One flan will need about 175ml / 6fl oz of double or whipping cream.

Lemon cheesecake

This is an easy recipe which does not require cooking and which freezes well.
It should be made a spring clip tin, 23cm to 25cm (9in to 10in) across.

Serves about 12.

300g / 10½oz crushed digestive biscuits
100g / 3½oz butter
Lemon jelly tablets or crystals, enough to set about 1.1ltr / 2pt water
280ml / ½pt water
50ml / 2fl oz lemon juice
550g / 1lb 4oz cream cheese
280ml / ½pt double cream

Method

Grease the bottom of the tin with a little butter.
Melt the butter in a pan and stir in the crushed biscuits.
Press the biscuit mixture into the base of the tin and leave to cool.

Dissolve the jelly in the water, add the lemon juice and leave it to cool. Do not allow it to start setting.
Whip the cream until it holds soft peaks.
Put the cream cheese in a bowl and gradually whisk in the cool jelly until the mixture is smooth.
Gently stir in the whipped cream, using a hand whisk, until well mixed.
Pour onto the biscuit base and smooth the top.
Leave in a refrigerator to set.

Run a knife round the inside of the tin to loosen it, unclip the sides and lift it off, leaving the cheesecake on the base of the tin.

The cheesecake can also be made in the following flavours:

Lime cheesecake

Follow the recipe for lemon cheesecake but use lime jelly instead of lemon.
Either lemon or fresh lime juice can be used.

Pineapple cheesecake

Follow the recipe for lemon cheesecake but use pineapple jelly instead of lemon.
Dissolve the jelly in 200ml / 7fl oz water instead of 280ml / ½pt.
Add 125ml / 4fl oz pineapple juice to the jelly instead of 50ml / 2fl oz lemon juice.

Strawberry or raspberry cheesecake

Follow the recipe for lemon cheesecake but use strawberry or raspberry jelly instead of lemon.
Dissolve the jelly in 200ml / 7fl oz water instead of 280ml / ½pt.
Add 125ml / 4fl oz strawberry or raspberry juice to the jelly instead of 50ml / 2fl oz lemon juice.
If plain strawberry or raspberry juice is not available, use a mixed juice like raspberry and orange, or raspberry and apple.

Tangerine cheesecake

Follow the recipe for lemon cheesecake but use tangerine jelly instead of lemon.
Dissolve the jelly in 200ml / 7fl oz water instead of 280ml / ½pt.
Add 125ml / 4fl oz orange or tangerine juice to the jelly instead of 50ml / 2fl oz lemon juice.

Notes on the recipe

Instead of using digestive biscuits, the base can be made from ginger nut biscuits, or a mixture of both. One method of crushing a large quantity of biscuits by hand is to put them in a strong plastic bag and break them up with a rolling pin. Or, put the biscuits in a big saucepan and crush them with the end of a rolling pin – if you have one that is flat at the ends.

The cheesecake looks attractive decorated with swirls of whipped cream and pieces of fruit. Because it is a rich dessert, the swirls of cream should be fairly small. For 12 portions of cheesecake, allow about 140ml / ¼pt of double or whipping cream.
For a suggested method of cutting a cheesecake into an uneven number of portions, see page 62.

The cheeseboard

A cheeseboard is a very popular extra course, especially at a formal evening meal. At a buffet, a cheeseboard can provide an alternative dessert for those who do not have a sweet tooth or are on a sugar free diet.

Cheese is usually served on a board or flat plate and people serve themselves using a special cheese knife. The cheeseboard should be large enough for the pieces of cheese to be attractively displayed along with a small bunch of grapes or another suitable decoration. At a sit-down meal it is easier for the guests if not more than six of them have to share one cheeseboard.

When the guests have finished with the cheeseboards and they have been cleared away, any leftover pieces of hard cheese can be grated and then frozen to use later in sandwiches, sauces or savoury toppings.

Suggested cheeseboard for 5 or 6 people

4 or 5 varieties of cheese each weighing about 100g / 3½oz
200g / 7oz of biscuits
85g / 3oz of butter
150g to 200g (5½oz to 7oz) of grapes

Preparing the cheeseboard

There should be variety in type and colour of cheese, though it is best to avoid a very soft cheese that is likely to spread into the others. A cheeseboard might include a hard cheese like Cheddar or Edam, a piece of Stilton, a piece of Brie, and one or two more unusual cheeses for people to try.

If you have to cut up large pieces of cheese on a regular basis it is worth buying a special cheese cutting board, which has a thin wire to slice through the cheese. It makes a neater cut than a knife, and is quicker to use.

Unwrapped pieces of cheese quickly dry out, so any cheeseboards prepared ahead must be suitably covered. Clean tea towels, soaked in cold water and then wrung out, will keep cheese moist.

Biscuits and butter

For each cheeseboard there should also be at least one plate of biscuits and a dish of butter. Cheese biscuits look more attractive arranged on a paper doily, but do not use a doily on a cheeseboard, as it will tend to stick to the cheese. It is better not to plate up the biscuits until shortly before they are needed, especially if you are working in a steamy kitchen, as they will soon start to lose their crispness.

Individual cheeseboards

When the cheese is served on individual plates, instead of larger boards, each plate should look similar. Three types of cheese for each person will give enough variety. As a finishing touch, put a tiny bunch of grapes or a piece of celery on each plate. Each person will also need a few biscuits and a portion of butter. These can either be put on the plates, or served separately.

Suggested individual cheeseboards for 10 people

3 varieties of cheese each weighing about 200g / 7oz
400g / 14oz of biscuits
150g / 5½oz of butter
400g / 14oz of grapes

Buffets

Most of the recipe sections in other parts of the book include dishes that are suitable for buffets.

A buffet is not always an easy option when you are catering for a large number of guests. Although a buffet usually involves less cooking than a sit-down meal, it is more difficult to calculate how much food is needed and how much time to allow for the meal. If the calculations are wrong, you can easily run short of food, or time, or both.

At a buffet, you need to prepare enough food to give the last guests in the queue the same choice as those at the front. Unfortunately, you cannot anticipate how much food people are going to take. Some pile their plates up, while others take only a small amount to leave plenty for those following on.

You need as much help at a large main meal buffet as you would for a sit-down dinner of a similar size. Buffet tables need supervision, plates and cutlery have to be cleared away after each course, and a large buffet produces an enormous amount of washing up.

Replenishing the buffet

Whatever the type of buffet, and whether it is a savoury or dessert course, the platters look best if they have plenty of food on them. The buffet table should never look as if it has been well 'picked over' before the last guests take their turn.

One way to make sure the buffet table always looks attractive is to keep replenishing the platters. At the beginning of the buffet, only put out about two thirds of the food. Then, as soon as a platter is half empty, bring a replacement from the kitchen, and take the depleted one back for refilling. In this way, the buffet table will always look well stocked, even if the platters gradually get smaller.

It is easier to replenish the platters and keep the buffet table tidy if those serving the buffet stand behind the table, and guests take their food from the front. It is also important that the people serving the buffet have quick and easy access to the kitchen.

It can be helpful for the guests if the dishes on the buffet table are labelled. This is not really necessary if the people serving the buffet have a good knowledge of what the various dishes contain. When there are labels dotted around the table, you have to be careful where you put each dish when replenishing the buffet.

Full meal buffet

This would normally include a main course and dessert, eaten with cutlery like a sit-down meal, and followed by coffee or tea. A full meal buffet is usually a cold meal, as it is easier to serve than a hot meal, especially if you are catering for a large number of people.

In theory, the wider the selection of food on offer, the less of each one you should need. In practice, people tend to copy each other and select similar items, and it is difficult to predict which ones they will choose. Cold meat is always popular, as are home-made pies and baked potatoes.

Flat plates or platters are suitable for displaying most types of food. Cold meat looks attractive arranged in overlapping slices on a platter. If possible, someone should serve the main dishes of the buffet, to control portion sizes, and answer any queries about the various dishes. One or two other people will also be needed to replenish the half empty platters and keep the buffet table tidy.

Guests at the buffet table are carrying a plate and serving themselves at the same time, so they need one-handed serving utensils. A large spoon or server is best for most dishes, but for salads and chunky foods like baked potatoes and chicken drumsticks, tongs are ideal.

Setting out the buffet

The buffet should flow along the table, starting with the empty plates. The main dishes of the buffet should be first in line, with salads and potatoes further along, and sauces and relishes at the far end. If bread rolls are offered as part of a buffet, it is usually better to put them on the dining tables. Otherwise, put them on a separate table, together with some butter, and small plates and knives. Those who want a bread roll can then help themselves without getting caught up in the queue for the main course.

The salt and pepper pots should be put on the dining tables, so guests can use them during the meal without having to come back to the buffet table. If the cutlery and napkins are not already in place on the tables, they can either be put near the plates, or somewhere near the end of the buffet.

Buffet service points

A buffet is slower to serve than a sit-down meal. If there are a large number of guests, it is possible for the first people in the queue to have finished eating before the last ones have started. Delays like this can be avoided by setting up several individual buffets or service points, each one having its own pile of empty plates and offering an identical choice of dishes. At each service point you need enough people to serve the main dishes and replenish the platters.

Guests should be asked to stay at their tables until invited to come up to the buffet. They can then be directed to a particular service point where the queue is shortest. This will help to ensure that everyone on a table can eat at about the same time. It will also prevent long queues developing, and keep people moving steadily through the buffet.

When there are fewer than 40 guests, unless there is considerable time pressure, one service point is adequate.

For parties of between 40 and 75, one long buffet table is ideal, with two service points and the plates at each end. The guests move from both ends of the table towards the middle. There should be two bowls of each sauce or relish in the middle of the table, with enough space around them to allow people coming from both sides to help themselves, and move away, without creating a bottle neck.

For larger numbers, having more service points will help to keep the queues short so no one has to wait too long for their meal.

If there is enough food left and time permits, many guests will enjoy a second helping. Some will probably come up for more without being invited! For this second wave, the food left on the platters can be rearranged to make an attractive, though smaller buffet, with fewer service points.

At this stage the redundant service points should be cleared away, or perhaps reorganised ready for the dessert course or coffee cups. If it is an informal occasion, someone can also start clearing the guests' empty plates.

Suggested savoury dishes for a cold full meal buffet

Cold roast beef, turkey and ham
Quiche and pork pies
Sausage meat and apple plait
Fresh salmon steaks
Tinned tuna and salmon
Stuffed eggs
Party mushrooms
Filled tomatoes
Rice salad
Coleslaw
Sausage and bean salad
Potato salad
Baked potatoes
Green salad

A selection of savoury dishes for a cold buffet might include two varieties of meat, quiches, pies, potatoes and three different salads, including a green salad. There should be a couple of dishes on the buffet table that are suitable for vegetarians.

Cold meat, fish, and items such as quiches and pies, should be served in fairly small pieces, so people can take a selection without overloading their plates.

Hot full meal buffet

A hot full meal buffet is more difficult to organise than a cold meal, and is difficult to serve satisfactorily without suitable equipment to keep the food hot. For smaller parties you can probably manage with a couple of hot trays, but if there is a second service point this becomes more difficult.

The amount of food that needs to be kept hot can be reduced by serving a green salad instead of vegetables. Baked potatoes are also useful, as they hold their heat for a long while, particularly if they are piled up in a deep dish.

At a hot buffet, people often prefer to sample a little food from two or three dishes, rather than taking one full sized helping. Because of this, larger pieces of meat like pork chops or chicken quarters are less suitable than dishes which are based around small pieces of meat or fish.

Suggested savoury dishes for a hot full meal buffet

Beef stew
Chicken drumsticks
Cottage pie
Chilli con carne
Sausage meat and apple plait
Vegetarian pastitsio
Baked potatoes
Green salad
Savoury rice

A selection of savoury dishes for a hot buffet might include two meat dishes, one vegetarian dish, a green salad and baked potatoes or rice.

Serving desserts at a buffet

A selection of about four desserts and a cheeseboard for each service point will give people plenty of choice.

A large dessert like a gateau looks splendid on a buffet table, but it needs someone competent to cut and serve it. A gateau is easier to cut into neat slices if the knife is dipped in and out of hot water between each slice. The hot water can be held in a tall jug beside the gateau.

Some small desserts, like fruit tartlets or meringues, look more attractive grouped together on a serving dish. Other desserts, like profiteroles, can be dished up onto individual plates before being put on the buffet table.

Hot desserts with custard are very popular, but because they soon cool down, they cannot be dished up in advance. To keep up with demand, you will probably need a fast moving person to carry the trays of pudding from cooker to buffet! Ice cream desserts are also popular, especially with children, but like hot puddings, you cannot dish them up more than a few minutes ahead.

Cheeseboard

Guests tend to take less cheese at a buffet than at a sit-down dinner. At each service point, one cheeseboard with butter and biscuits, and one in reserve, is usually sufficient. As soon as a cheeseboard starts to look depleted it should be replaced.

Not as many service points are needed for the desserts, because people do not usually follow one another along the table. Putting a large dessert like a gateau at one end, a cheeseboard and fruit bowl at the opposite end, with two or three other desserts in the middle, usually works well. Any dessert that is not already plated up will need some empty plates next to it. As well as the desserts, you may also need one or two jugs of cream and some custard for any hot puddings. If it is a full meal buffet, the dessert cutlery can either be laid up on the dining tables or fetched from the buffet area.

Suggested desserts for a buffet

Pineapple upside down sponge
Gateaux
Profiteroles with chocolate sauce
Fruit tartlets
Individual sherry trifles
Meringues
Fresh fruit salad
Fruit spongc flan
Lemon cheesecake
Fruit bowl
Cheeseboard

Finger buffet

This type of buffet varies from a savoury snack to a much more elaborate two course meal, which could include some quite substantial items. The dishes should be suitable to eat with the fingers and not be too sticky or greasy.

A finger buffet can be organised in a similar way to a full meal buffet, although it is quicker to serve and so you need fewer service points. Although guests are helping themselves, people are still needed behind the buffet table to replenish the platters, answer questions about the dishes, and deal with any problems that might arise.

If you are serving a finger buffet where there are a large number of children amongst the guests, it is particularly important that the buffet table is properly supervised. Excited children can quickly cause havoc at a buffet if their parents are not watching them.

In some situations, several people may get together to provide the food for a finger buffet, each bringing something they prepared at home. In this case, if each dish is different, it is better to put everything out on the buffet table at the beginning, and not keep things back for replenishing. There should still be someone at the buffet table to remove the empty platters and keep the buffet looking presentable.

Suggested finger buffet menu for 50 guests

Sandwiches	3 large loaves
Chicken drumsticks	60
Medium sized sausage rolls	60
Pizza	approx. 3.3kg / 7lb 8oz
Quiche	approx. 3.3kg / 7lb 8oz
Cocktail sausages on sticks	2kg / 4lb 8oz
Pork pies	4.5kg / 10lb
Vol-au-vents	75
Crisps	400g
Cheese and pineapple on sticks	60
Celery boats	60

A finger buffet is more interesting if some of the food, for example, sausage rolls and sausages on sticks, can be served hot. To save time at the last minute, they can be cooked and arranged on platters a short while before the meal, and then put back into the oven to heat through.

When serving a two course finger buffet, the desserts could either be similar to those for a main meal buffet, or you could continue the finger buffet theme by providing a selection of small cakes and desserts that can be eaten without cutlery.

Sandwiches

Large (800g) rectangular, medium-sliced loaves contain between 18 and 20 slices and are the easiest to use when making a large quantity of sandwiches. For each loaf you need about 150g / 5½oz of soft spread margarine or butter.

Each of these fillings is enough for one large loaf of sandwiches:
400g / 14oz tinned tuna or salmon mixed with a little mayonnaise
500g / 1lb 2oz sliced cold meat
350g / 12oz grated cheese
8 hard boiled eggs mashed with a little mayonnaise or salad cream

To quickly mash a large quantity of shelled hard boiled eggs, first break them up on a cheese grater, then add the salad cream or mayonnaise, and finally finish them off with a potato masher.

Making sandwiches

When making a large number of sandwiches, it is much quicker to do them in bulk rather than one at a time. Start by buttering all the bread. Put the buttered sides loosely together in pairs and stack them one above another.

Fill all the rounds of buttered bread, again stacking them in piles. Finally, cut the sandwiches into neat triangles, doing several rounds at a time using a serrated knife with a long blade. Each large loaf will make between 36 and 40 small triangular sandwiches.

Sandwiches look attractive arranged in rows on a platter, with their points uppermost. If the rows of sandwiches slope back a little, individual sandwiches can be easily removed without disturbing the rest. The platters can be garnished with cucumber and tomato, some sprigs of parsley, and a sprinkling of cress.

Once a loaf of bread has been unwrapped it quickly dries out. Sliced bread and platters of sandwiches can be kept moist by covering them with tea towels that have been soaked in cold water and then wrung out.

Vol-au-vents

Vol-au-vents are always popular and the ready made frozen cases which are bought uncooked are quite satisfactory and save a lot of time and effort.

Mushroom vol-au-vents

Makes about 30 medium sized vol-au-vents.

225g / 8oz mushrooms, finely chopped
100g / 3½oz butter
70g / 2½oz flour (plain or self-raising)
500g / 1lb 2oz mushroom soup (approx)
pinch of salt and pepper
large pinch of mace

Method

Melt the butter in a saucepan and gently fry the chopped mushrooms until soft.
Stir in the flour, and gradually add enough soup to make a very thick sauce.
Add the seasonings.
Spoon the filling into the cooked pastry cases.
Serve at once, or leave to cool, and reheat as required.

Prawn vol-au-vents

Makes about 30 medium sized vol-au-vents.

450g / 1lb shelled prawns*
280g / 10oz mayonnaise
15ml / 1 tablespoon tomato ketchup

***If using frozen prawns, the weight is after defrosting and draining.**

Method

Mix all the ingredients together and spoon the filling into the cooked pastry cases.

Vegetarian meals and special diets

When catering for the same group of people on a regular basis, you get to know who is vegetarian, or on a special diet, and can therefore plan ahead. On other occasions, especially if the guests are having a set meal, it is important to have an alternative that is suitable for vegetarians and can be served at short notice. Even if people have been asked to let you know in advance if they require a special meal, the message does not always get through, or they forget to tell you, so you need to prepare for the unexpected.

Most vegetarians will not eat any meat or fish. Others interpret the term more loosely, and although they do not eat meat, they will eat fish or shellfish. Occasionally a person who eats meat will suddenly decide to become 'vegetarian' when they see an attractive looking vegetarian dish being served to someone else on the table! It is therefore a good idea to serve the vegetarian meals last.

Guests who are on a gluten free diet or who are vegan are likely to contact you beforehand to discuss the menu. In these cases, it is important to find out exactly what alternative meal would be acceptable.

Nut allergies

Because of the increasing number of people suffering from nut allergies, guests should always be informed if any dishes contain nuts. This is simple to do when there is a choice of dishes with a written menu. At a buffet, any dishes containing nuts should be clearly labelled. At a set meal, it is safer to leave nuts off the menu.

Low fat diets

Semi-skimmed milk and low fat spread should be available for anyone who wants to limit their fat intake. If dairy cream is on the menu, low fat yoghurt could be offered as an alternative. A dessert based around fresh fruit is usually suitable for this group of people, and if it is made without sugar, it can also be served to people with diabetes and those on a low calorie diet. It is also useful to have some artificial sweeteners available in both powder and tablet form.

Both the following vegetarian recipes can be made in either single portion ovenproof dishes or larger ones as part of a hot buffet. The oven temperature and timings are not critical, as long as they are served hot. They can both be made the day before and refrigerated, and they also freeze well.

Cashew and parsnip roast

This recipe is an unusual and delicious combination of parsnips and cashew nuts. For easier portion control it should be made in dishes that are about 6cm / 2½in deep.

Makes about 15 portions as a main course.

1 kg / 2lb 4oz roughly chopped parsnips
170g / 6oz butter
280ml / ½pt well flavoured vegetable stock
900g / 2lb chopped cashew nuts
225g / 8oz soft brown breadcrumbs
3 beaten eggs
7.5ml / 1 level dessertspoon rosemary
7.5ml / 1 level dessertspoon thyme
¼ teaspoon salt and pepper

75ml / 3fl oz cooking oil
500g / 1lb 2oz finely chopped onions
6 crushed cloves garlic
800g / 1lb 12oz chopped mushrooms

Method

Boil the parsnips until very soft then mash them with about half the butter.
Add the stock, chopped nuts, breadcrumbs, beaten eggs, herbs and seasoning.
Stir thoroughly and leave on one side.

Heat the oil and remaining butter in a frying pan, and fry the onions and garlic for about 2 min.
Add the mushrooms and fry gently until the onions and mushrooms are soft.
Strain off any liquid and add it to the parsnip mixture, stirring well.

Using about half the parsnip mixture, put some in the bottom of each dish.
Divide the mushrooms and onions between the dishes to make a middle layer.
Spread the rest of the parsnip mixture on top.
Cover the dishes with foil, and bake at 180°C, 350°F, gas mark 4 for about 1 hr, removing the foil for the last 20 min of cooking time.

Notes on the recipe

If possible, use both plain, and roasted salted cashew nuts, in roughly equal proportions.
It does not matter if the nuts are not chopped evenly. If they are done in a food processer and some turn to grounds while others are still whole, it will not spoil the dish.

Vegetable pastitsio

This is a very tasty dish, and would be suitable as a vegetarian alternative at a set meal, or as part of a hot buffet. For easier portion control it should be made in dishes that are about 6cm / 2½in deep.

Makes about 10 portions as a main course.

75ml / 3fl oz oil for frying
400g / 14oz finely chopped onions
4 crushed cloves garlic
1.6kg / 3lb 9oz tinned chopped tomatoes*
225g / 8oz red lentils
70g / 2½oz tomato ketchup (approx)
1 heaped teaspoon cinnamon
1 heaped teaspoon oregano
225g / 8oz pasta shells or bows
100g / 3½oz butter
50g / 2oz flour
550ml / 1pt milk
300g / 10½oz thinly sliced mushrooms
140g / 5oz grated Cheddar

*** Some brands of tinned tomato have a stronger flavour than others. It is worth tasting the tomato mixture before it goes in the dishes, and if it is not quite strong enough, add some more tomato ketchup.**

Method

Heat the oil in a saucepan and gently fry the onions and garlic for 5 min.
Strain the tomatoes, leave on one side, and add the liquid from the tins to the pan.
Rinse the lentils and add to the pan.
Cover and cook until the lentils are soft, adding a little water if necessary.
Add the tomatoes, tomato ketchup, cinnamon and oregano.
Cook uncovered to evaporate some of the liquid until the mixture has the consistency of porridge.
If necessary, add a little more tomato ketchup.

Meanwhile cook the pasta shapes until tender, drain them.
Make a white sauce from the butter, flour and milk.

Using about half the tomato mixture, put some in the bottom of each dish.
Divide up the pasta between the dishes.
Put the rest of the tomato mixture on top of the pasta.
Put a layer of mushrooms in each dish on top of the tomato mixture.
Pour the white sauce over the mushrooms.
Sprinkle with grated cheese and cook in a fairly hot oven 200°C, 400°F, gas mark 6 for about 45 min or until hot and golden brown.

After dinner coffee

Coffee is usually served at the end of the meal and provides the signal for a slowing down of pace towards the final phase of the occasion, whether it is informal conversation or more formal speeches.

Unless the dessert course is followed by a cheeseboard, coffee is normally served once the desserts have been cleared. It is important to start pouring coffee fairly promptly, particularly at an evening dinner, or people will start to leave their places to go to the bar, the toilet or to chat to friends on other tables. If there is a cheeseboard, serve it first and then pour coffee.

Unless you have access to a suitable machine, it is difficult to make a large quantity of ground coffee in a short space of time. Because of this, it is usually best to concentrate on speed and convenience and use a quality brand of instant coffee.

The water boiler

It is important to make sure that when the time comes to serve coffee, there is sufficient boiling water. This is no problem if the water boiler is plumbed in. If you are using an 'older style' water boiler, it is a good idea to boil it up shortly before the meal, and then turn it off. If the kitchen is then so hectic that you forget about coffee and are late switching the boiler on, it is not having to heat up from cold.

Unless the boiler holds sufficient water for all the guests, it is useful to have a large kettle as a standby. If the boiler is going to need refilling while you are pouring coffee, it is best not to wait until it is empty or it will take too long to reheat. If you refill the boiler while it is still about one third full, it will soon boil up again.

Milk and sugar

The individual portions of UHT milk have their uses, but little jugs of fresh milk look more attractive on the tables. Sugar sachets, however, are a practical and acceptable alternative to loose sugar. They are not as messy, and allow people to choose white or brown sugar, or artificial sweeteners, without having separate bowls. If after dinner chocolates are offered, they should be served on small plates, rather than on the coffee saucers where the heat from the cups will melt them.

Coffee poured at the tables

Coffee cups should not be put out before the meal. They take up valuable space and spoil the look of the tables. Instead, arrange the cups and saucers, sugar bowls and empty milk jugs on trays, using one for each table and numbering them to match. These trays can be left on one side until people are eating their dessert course. The milk jugs can then be filled and the trays taken to the tables.

When coffee is poured at the table, people should be asked whether they would like it black or white, and have their cups filled accordingly. When pouring coffee, a waiting cloth or clean white tea towel held under the spout, will catch any drips.

Some people will probably request decaffeinated coffee, so this should always be available. It is a good idea to make sure any jars of decaffeinated coffee are clearly labelled, so no one uses them by mistake. If anyone requests tea, the best option is to take them a small pot so they can pour their own. Occasionally someone might ask for herbal tea, a mug of hot chocolate or a glass of milk.

After serving the first round of coffee, if time permits, people usually appreciate the offer of a second cup. If there are sufficient coffee pots you may be able to leave one on each table for people to serve themselves. This is especially welcome if there are speeches after the meal.

Coffee served in the cups

Even though the empty cups and saucers are not going to be taken to the tables, it will save time later if they are put on trays before the meal. They should be arranged singly, and not piled up.

When it is time to serve the coffee, the quickest method is to make it in a large pot or jug and pour it from there into the cups. If this is not convenient, the coffee powder can be put in each cup, and the hot water added from a large pot or jug. Either method is quicker and safer than holding each cup individually under the nozzle of the water boiler.

The milk can be poured into the cups before they leave the kitchen, keeping one or two cups of black coffee on each tray. Alternatively, the milk can be served in jugs on the tables, which gives the guests more choice. The sugar, even if you are using sachets, should always be put in bowls on the tables rather than on the coffee saucers.

Guide to quantities - for 20 people allowing 1 cup each

Instant coffee	40g / 1½oz
Tea (in large pots)	12 teabags
Milk	550ml / 1pt
Loose sugar	About 300g / 10½oz depending on the number of sugar bowls

The Christmas dinner

The success of a Christmas dinner relies more on traditional good cheer than on an imaginative menu. With a festive atmosphere, cheerful table decorations and a welcoming drink, people will be enjoying themselves long before the turkey arrives!

A traditional Christmas meal is not very different from most other types of roast dinner. However, because of the importance of the occasion, cooking it can be quite stressful. This is particularly true if the oven is not large enough. As a general rule, it is better to keep a Christmas dinner as simple as possible, rather than trying to produce something elaborate especially for the occasion.

The first course

If you are serving a first course, a prawn cocktail *(page 44)* or a melon boat with Christmas sails *(page 48)* would be a good choice. Most of the preparation can be done in advance, and both starters look very attractive on the table. Soup is always popular, but it lacks visual impact, and might be too filling before a heavy main course. There also has to be sufficient space on top of the cooker for the soup pan.

The main course

A possible choice for the main course might be:

roast turkey (boneless breast)
chipolata sausage
sage and onion stuffing
roast potatoes
mashed potatoes
carrots
Brussels sprouts
gravy
cranberry sauce

The turkey must be thoroughly cooked to avoid any chance of food poisoning. A temperature of at least 78°C in the thickest part of the joint is recommended. As soon as enough juices have come off the turkey, the gravy can be made, saving time later.

If the oven is not large enough to take everything at once, the chipolatas and stuffing balls can be cooked ahead, when the turkey first goes in. Once they are cooked, cool them a little, and then pile them up in deeper dishes under foil for reheating later. This will leave more room in the oven for the trays of roast potatoes. If you are reheating food, it should be tested with a temperature probe before dishing up to make sure it is over 75°C *(page 128)*.

When space is short, the floor of the cooker, under the bottom shelf, can sometimes be used for cooking or reheating food. The oven floor of some electric cookers can even get hot enough to produce crispy roast potatoes.

If there is a shortage of space on top of the cooker, or not enough large pans, the sprouts and carrots can share one pan. Cook the sprouts until they are still slightly firm, and then strain them into a large colander and cover them with a lid. Cook the carrots in the same pan, with the colander of sprouts supported across the top. The sprouts will keep hot and continue to cook slowly over the carrots. If the sprouts are not fully cooked by the time they are needed, strain off the carrots and give the sprouts a few minutes in a little boiling water in the bottom of the pan.

Christmas puddings

Allow about 120g / 4oz of Christmas pudding per person.

The flimsy film lids that cover some bought puddings can sometimes split around the edges during reheating. As a precaution, to prevent steam getting in, it is advisable to cover these puddings with foil before reheating.

To reheat puddings in the oven, stand them in about 2.5cm / 1in of water in a deep roasting tin, and cover the tin with foil. If the pudding basins are plastic, do not allow them to touch the edges of the roasting tin, or they might start to melt.

To reheat puddings on top of the cooker, stack them on a trivet in a saucepan which has about 5cm / 2in of water in the bottom. Depending on the size of the saucepan, a small baking tin, or a pan lid could be used as a trivet. It should be sufficiently large to lift the puddings off the base of the pan and away from the heat source. Bring the water to simmering point and cover the pan to enclose the steam. Rotate the puddings from time to time, so they heat evenly.

Whether the puddings are reheated inside the oven, or on top, they will need regular checking to make sure the water does not boil dry.

Custard and brandy cream

Some people like plain custard with their Christmas pudding, while others prefer something stronger. Brandy cream is easy to make and very popular. It is best served in small bowls so guests can help themselves.

For notes on custard see page 83. When there is a shortage of either pans or space on the cooker, instant custard can be made straight into a measuring jug as required.

Brandy cream - to serve about 10 people.

Whip up about 225ml / 8fl oz of double or whipping cream and stir in 7.5ml / 1 dessertspoon of sifted icing sugar and the same of brandy.

Crackers and novelties

If there are Christmas crackers on the tables, people usually pull them before or during the first course. Collecting up the discarded crackers will prevent them getting into the food, and keep the tables looking tidy for the rest of the meal. If you are offering dishes of novelties, it is generally better to put them out towards the end of the meal.

Afternoon tea

For notes on calculating quantities of sandwiches and other savoury items, see Buffets, page 102.

Afternoon tea is often served as part of another function or event, such as a birthday celebration or Christening, and is usually a more leisurely meal than a lunch or dinner. One of the most important elements of an afternoon tea is the tea itself, which needs to be freshly brewed and quickly available. There should be sufficient tea for people to have a second or third cup if they wish, with coffee and fruit juice as an alternative. Once the tea has been poured, the rest of the meal can follow at a slower pace.

Afternoon tea would normally include some dainty sandwiches, a couple of savoury items, biscuits or scones, and cake. It is a relatively straightforward meal to organise, and does not require much kitchen help. The amount of food required is not difficult to calculate, and most tea-time recipes can be easily expanded into quantities suitable for larger numbers.

Cakes

Whether or not sandwiches and scones are being offered, cakes are essential at an afternoon tea. The type of cakes served will depend upon the occasion and the budget. The choice of cakes is important, and if you have only allowed one for each guest, they should all be of a similar type. It is asking for trouble to include just a few cream cakes amongst a platter of plain ones!

Large cakes, once they have been cut, can soon become dry, so it is advisable to leave slicing them until shortly before service, or cover the platters with cling film. If there are a lot of guests, it is often quicker and easier to offer a selection of small cakes. Fairy cakes are a good choice, as they are simple to make, portion control is easy, and they can be flavoured and decorated in various ways. The plain sponge recipe on page 85 will make between 80 and 100 small fairy cakes.

Afternoon tea can be served as a buffet, as a sit-down meal, or as a combination of the two, with the food displayed on the buffet table, and the drinks served to the guests. Afternoon tea is not usually served as a plated meal.

Afternoon tea as a buffet

When afternoon tea is served as a buffet, you require fewer tea pots, milk jugs and sugar bowls than at a sit-down meal. You can also display a wider selection of dishes. However, carrying a plate of food from the buffet table can be difficult for guests with limited mobility, especially if they are expected to carry a cup of tea at the same time. If there are a number of elderly people amongst the guests, it is helpful if someone can assist with bringing cups of tea to the tables.

The tea is usually poured at one end of the buffet table, with the cups, milk jug and sugar bowl nearby. If there are two people pouring tea it speeds up service, and one tea pot can still be in use while the other is being refilled. Some catering sized teapots require two hands to pour them. To avoid scalds when using large teapots, it is safer to pour into the cups while they are still on the buffet table, rather than being held.

The dessert plates and napkins can either be placed at the other end of the buffet table, or stacked at intervals along the table, so there is less queuing. In this arrangement, the food should be displayed so there is a good selection of dishes near each pile of plates.

At an afternoon tea, as with any buffet, there should be sufficient people behind the buffet table to replenish the platters and answer any questions about the dishes.

Afternoon tea as a sit-down meal

If most of the guests are elderly, it is probably easier for everyone if the meal is served at the tables. If there are enough teapots of a suitable size, people can pour their own tea. These teapots will need frequent refilling. You need plenty of milk jugs and sugar bowls on the tables, at least one between six.

If the teapots are very large, and therefore not suitable for the guests to use, it might be possible for someone to go around the tables pouring tea. This can take a while, as most people prefer to put their milk in first, and requests for coffee or soft drinks will cause further delays. If the teapots are all catering sized, they are likely to be too large to use safely at the tables, so the cups will have to be filled in the kitchen and taken out on trays.

The plates of sandwiches and cakes must not be so large that they are awkward to pass around the table. Those that serve up to six people are a good size. For instance, if there are ten guests on the table, there should be a plate of sandwiches at each end, rather than one large platter in the middle which only a few people can reach.

Afternoon tea is sometimes served in two courses. The savoury dishes are served first, and as they are cleared away, the cakes and other sweet things are brought out. This is a good system if you are short of space on the tables. If there is plenty of space, the savoury and sweet dishes can all be put out at the same time. People then know from the start of the meal exactly what is being provided, and can make their choices accordingly.

Suggested dishes for an afternoon tea

Sandwiches
Sausage rolls
Sausage on sticks
Cheese and pineapple on sticks
Vol-au-vents
Scones
Sweet biscuits
Buttered fruit loaf
Fairy cakes
Cream cakes

Accompaniments

Items such as bread rolls, butter and cold sauces, although not as significant as the main dishes, still make an important contribution to the enjoyment of the meal. When attractively presented, these accompaniments can enhance not only the food, but also the overall appearance of the dining table.

It is inconvenient if people have to stretch right across a large table to reach, for example, the butter or salt. It is just as unsatisfactory if the butter or salt has to be passed from one end of the table to the other. Because of this, it is a good rule not to expect more than six people to share items such as a basket of rolls, a dish of butter, or a bowl of mayonnaise. Taking butter as an example, a table of between seven and twelve guests should be given at least two dishes.

Bread rolls

Most people expect to be offered a bread roll with their first course. Having a selection of rolls in a basket or bowl gives them a choice and is far preferable to leaving a roll on each side plate. If you are using wicker baskets, they should be lined with a napkin or doily. Baskets made from synthetic materials which can be washed do not need to be lined.

If the rolls are served in baskets for people to help themselves, allowing one roll per person plus a couple extra for each table is usually adequate. You also need a few spare rolls in case anyone asks for more.

If you offer bread instead of rolls, it is better not to slice it until shortly before the meal, as it soon dries out. You can help to prevent it drying out by covering it with cling film. Spare pieces of sliced bread can be kept in a covered container or saucepan.

Butter

For bread rolls, jacket potatoes or biscuits for cheese, allow about 150g / 5½oz of butter for every 10 people. A low fat alternative to butter should also be available for anyone who requests it.

Small wrapped portions of butter are very convenient, but not as attractive as a dish of decorative butter curls. A metal butter curler works best if you dip it into very hot water before dragging it across the butter. The butter is easier to work with when it is very cold.

If you are not making butter curls, the butter can simply be cut into small, neat pieces and arranged in a dish.

Using a butter curler

Salt and pepper

Matching salt and pepper pots look smart and help to give the tables a coordinated appearance. Unfortunately, when catering for large numbers, you often have to make do with salt and pepper pots of varying shapes and sizes, some matching and some not. In this situation, it is best to forget about the whole room, and simply try to have matching sets on each table. Any odd sets can be used singly on small tables, or as an extra set in the middle of a large one.

All the salt and pepper pots should be checked before the meal to make sure they are well filled and the holes are not blocked. At the same time, any smears or finger marks can be wiped off. Although it only takes a few minutes to do a routine check like this, it is a task that is often overlooked.

Salt can quickly become damp, so it is important that it is stored in a dry place. If you are in any doubt about the condition of the salt, check it before the meal by shaking a little out of each pot.

Mustard

It is worth keeping a small jar of English and French mustard in stock, in case anyone requests it. It is not usually necessary to put mustard on the dining tables.

Cold sauces

If you are using commercial sauces rather than home-made, it is worth buying a reputable brand that the guests will like, rather than risk giving them a cheap substitute.

Cold sauces should be served in a small dish or bowl, preferably on a saucer to catch any spills. If possible, the saucer should be wide enough to support a teaspoon.

People vary a great deal in how much sauce they take, making it difficult to calculate how much to provide. These quantities of sauce should be enough for about 10 people at a sit-down meal:

Apple sauce: 300g / 10½oz

Cranberry sauce: 200g / 7oz

Horseradish sauce: 150g / 5½oz

Mayonnaise: 200g / 7oz

Mayonnaise and horseradish sauce soon begin to dry out once they are taken out of the jar, so it is better not to dish them up more than twenty minutes before the meal.

Mayonnaise is extremely useful in the kitchen – it is so versatile.
Mix it with a little tomato ketchup to make a seafood sauce.
Shake it up with vinaigrette for a delicious salad dressing.
Stir some mustard into it and you have a spicy dip
…and so on!

Drinks

When it comes to enjoying the occasion, the drinks are less important than the food. On the whole, people will enjoy drinking whatever you provide.

The main challenge with the drinks is trying to estimate how much you need. It is also easy to overlook their bulk and weight when shopping for a large party. Keeping drinks chilled can also be a problem, especially if the party is in a hired room or marquee.

The bar

If you are providing drinks for no more than eighty guests, you can set up a suitable drinks table or bar from two or three long tables (approx. 3.6m / 12ft total length) covered with wipeable banquet roll or plastic tablecloths. To reduce the risk of accidental spillage, it is important that the tables are the same height, free from wobbles, and ideally, secured together. If the bar is covered in a similar way to a buffet table *(page 15)* it will look smart and give space for reserve bottles and glasses to be stored underneath.

The bar should be positioned so the guests have easy access to the front. Anyone helping on the bar will also need access around the back so they can get at the spare bottles and glasses. It looks better if you have just a few opened bottles of each drink on show on the bar, with the replenishment bottles out of sight. If there is no refrigerator, bottles that need to be chilled can be held in plastic boxes containing ice cubes and cold water. Bags of ice cubes from a supermarket are cheap, hygienic and easy to use. Bottles taken from these chilled boxes are slippery so should be dried before being put out on the bar.

Organising the drinks

At a large party, it is very useful to have some help with the drinks. For a party of fifty people, three helpers should be able to keep the bar tidy and replenished, pour drinks where necessary, and collect and wash the dirty glasses. It is worth giving some thought as to where the glasses will be washed. If the sink is some distance from the bar you will need some trays to transport dirty glasses for washing, and bring back the clean ones.

At a large dinner or party, collecting empty glasses on a regular basis reduces the chance of breakages and leaves less work to do when the guests have gone. Small, non-slip trays that can be carried in one hand are ideal for collecting empty glasses. Using a tray is preferable to people putting their fingers inside the glasses to carry them. It looks unattractive and is unhygienic, and sometimes a guest may not have quite finished their drink, or may wish to keep their glass for a refill.

The glasses

It is easy to underestimate the number of glasses you need. Guests who start with a glass of wine may later change to beer or soft drinks. At a lively party when the room is full, glasses get mixed up, and mislaid, and people come for a new one rather than risk taking someone else's drink. As a guideline, allow three wine glasses and two half pint glasses per person for a party of both men and women. Goblet shaped half pint glasses are the most suitable for soft drinks, and the longer the party goes on, the more you are likely to need.

If you are serving pints of beer, sparkling wine or sherry, you will obviously need different glasses. When champagne is served, one saucer or flute glass for each person is usually sufficient.

Glasses can often be borrowed free from the supermarket which sells you the drink. Before using them, it is worth giving them a thorough wash to make sure any dust or traces of lipstick have been removed. When drying the glasses you can also check them for cracks and chips.

Plastic glasses are a possible option, and may be stipulated at some venues, especially at outdoor events where broken glass could prove dangerous. While the cost of individual plastic glasses is low, they are often single-use, so could work out expensive for a large party. Another difficulty with these glasses is that they tend to be available only in a limited range of shapes and sizes. A good quality drink can lose its impact if it is served in a plastic glass.

What drinks to serve?

The choice of drink should reflect the likely drinking habits of the guests. It should also be compatible with the available glasses, just as the menu has to suit the crockery and cutlery. There may also be financial considerations when deciding what drinks to serve.

It is generally better to restrict the choice of drinks, but have enough of each to avoid running out of the ones that prove most popular. Many supermarkets will sell drink on a sale or return basis which can be useful.

Beer, lager, red and white wine are solid choices for alcoholic drinks. Wine is easier to deal with if it comes in screw top bottles, which have now lost their 'down market' image. Lemonade is very useful as it can be mixed with other drinks to reduce the alcohol content. Cola and fruit drinks are usually popular, as is bottled water, especially amongst younger people. These drinks are easier to pour if the bottles are no larger than one litre.

If it seems likely that a number of guests may prefer a non-alcoholic drink, then a home-made fruit cup may be a good choice. It could either be decorated with small pieces of fruit and sliced cucumber, or you could make miniature fruit 'kebabs' on cocktail sticks, and place one in each glass.

When the initial drink is served, people can be told what drinks are available, and whether they are expected to help themselves when they want a refill.

How much to buy?

Even when you know how many people are coming to a party, it can be difficult to decide how much drink to buy. People will usually drink more in the evening than at a lunchtime or afternoon party. When they are arriving in couples by car, you will need fewer alcoholic drinks and more soft drinks than if they are walking to the venue or coming by coach.

When a party is for elderly people, you will probably need more medium/sweet white wine, than red. If there are younger people present, the emphasis will probably be on red wine.

Suggested drinks for a family party of about fifty people

8 bottles red wine
8 bottles white wine
8 doz cans lager
2 doz cans beer
2 doz cans cider
10 ltr lemonade
10 ltr cola
10 ltr fruit juice or carbonated fruit drink
10 ltr bottled water

Wine with the meal

At a sit-down lunch or dinner, the wine can either be poured, or the bottles left on the tables for people to help themselves, or you can do both.

A good system, especially if the wine supply is limited, is to pour each guest their first glass of wine, and then leave the bottle on the table. This ensures that everyone is given a glass of wine, without the risk of running out while pouring refill glasses. It is much quicker and easier to pour the wine if people are only given a choice from two bottles.

You can expect to get about six glasses of wine from a normal (75cl) bottle. As a guide, one bottle should serve three people at a meal. People who are not drinking wine with their meal will appreciate having a jug or bottle of water on the table.

Other suggestions for drinks

The following ideas may be helpful if you wish to go a little more 'up market' and yet still manage the drinks yourself:

Champagne

It enjoys the reputation of being the ultimate celebration drink, but from a practical standpoint it suffers from several snags. Champagne is expensive, usually very dry, needs chilling and is difficult for the amateur to open and pour without danger and waste. Many people feel that good sparkling wine offers better value than cheap champagne, and has a wider sweetness range to suit all tastes.

When opening a bottle of champagne or sparkling wine, point the bottle away from any guests, windows or ornaments. Hold the cork in the bottle while removing the wire cage, and then turn the bottle to open the wine. Have a glass to hand, so you can start pouring immediately. You should be able to get six glasses out of a bottle of champagne, whether it is served in a flute, or saucer shaped glass.

Buck's Fizz

This is half champagne or sparkling wine, and half chilled orange juice. It is named after a London club where it was invented in 1921 as an excuse to begin drinking early! It is popular in summer, being more refreshing than straight wine. From an economic standpoint, Buck's Fizz is an attractive proposition, as, despite its grandiose title, the wine will go twice as far. When pouring Buck's Fizz, always pour the wine into the glass before the orange juice. The two mix much better than the other way round.

Wine cup

An attractive wine cup, decorated with sliced fruit, is usually a very popular choice. There are many recipes for making a wine cup, but if you decide to base it on surplus bottles of wine left over from previous occasions, it is unlikely that anyone will complain. The ingredients in the wine cup do not need to stay exactly the same throughout the party. However, the alcohol content and colour should remain constant, so the cup always looks the same and guests know how much they are drinking. A good guide is to make the wine cup about half as strong as wine.

Pimms, or one of its alternatives, makes a quick and easy base for a summer cup. Dilute it with three parts lemonade or dry ginger, and serve chilled, decorated with small pieces of fruit and sprigs of mint.

Food safety

Everyone has the right to enjoy a meal without becoming ill, and it is the responsibility of food handlers, whether or not they are being paid, to make sure the meals they serve are safe to eat. Elderly people and children are particularly vulnerable where food poisoning is concerned, and in some cases the symptoms and consequences can be life-threatening.

Problems with food safety can easily arise when different groups of people use the same kitchen, and no one has overall responsibility for cleaning or looking after it. If the kitchen and equipment are not cleaned on a regular basis, dirt and food debris can build up in awkward to reach places, attracting food pests and harmful bacteria.

Maintaining a high standard of food safety is relatively straightforward in a well appointed catering kitchen with trained staff and proper supervision. It is much more of a challenge when you are trying to produce a large dinner in an unfamiliar, poorly equipped kitchen.

Food poisoning

The foods most commonly involved in outbreaks of food poisoning include:

meat, especially poultry
milk, cream and dairy products
rice
fish and shellfish
eggs and egg products
gravy and sauces.

These items are likely to feature on the menu of a large sit-down meal or buffet.

Many people mistakenly believe they can tell if food is safe by how it looks and smells. Although it is easy to recognise when food is going off and is therefore unsuitable to eat, a meal containing food poisoning bacteria can look, taste and smell quite normal. The only way to discover if it is harmful is by looking at it under a microscope.

Food poisoning is usually caused by eating food that is contaminated with large numbers of harmful bacteria. These bacteria are sometimes present in raw food when it comes into the kitchen, as for example, in meat, fish and eggs. Because of this, raw food should be kept well away from cooked food.

Harmful bacteria are also found in the soil that clings to the skin and outer leaves of vegetables. Waste food, particularly raw meat and vegetable trimmings should always be disposed of in a bin away from other food.

Domestic pets and food pests such as rodents and flies carry harmful bacteria, so they should be kept out of the kitchen.

Many healthy people carry food poisoning bacteria on their skin and hair, and in their throats, without any ill effects. It is therefore important not to handle food with unwashed hands, or cough or sneeze over food.

How bacteria reproduce

Bacteria are single celled organisms which reproduce by dividing in half, each parent cell producing two identical offspring. In order to divide, bacteria need a food source. Most bacteria prefer high protein, moist food. They cannot reproduce in food that is completely dry.

Warmth is another requirement for bacterial reproduction. Most food poisoning bacteria can divide at temperatures between 5°C and 63°C, though their preferred temperature is around 37°C, the same as the human body.

In favourable conditions, for example, on moist high protein food in a warm room, bacteria take between ten and twenty minutes to divide. In this situation, in a matter of hours, a small number of bacteria can increase to several million, probably enough to cause food poisoning.

Destroying bacteria

Most bacteria that are present in food will be killed by normal cooking temperatures. It is usually recommended that the temperature in the thickest part of the joint, or centre of the food, should reach at least 75°C.

In the kitchen, bacteria can be reduced to a safe level by disinfection. This can be done with either an anti-bacterial disinfectant, or very hot water, 82°C or above. As a general rule, anything in the kitchen that has frequent contact with food or with people's hands should be disinfected, along with kitchen cloths, mops, and the waste food bin.

High risk food

High risk food describes any ready-to-eat, high protein, moist food. When high protein food has been cooked, it becomes high risk and needs careful handling to prevent contamination by harmful bacteria. This is because it is unlikely to be heated again to a temperature that will destroy bacteria. Therefore, if any food poisoning bacteria manage to contaminate high risk food, they will probably survive, and given the right conditions, start to reproduce.

High risk food includes many dishes found on a buffet table, for example: cold meat, shellfish, sausage rolls, chicken drumsticks, quiches, sausages on sticks, pork pies and sandwiches. High risk desserts include cheesecake, gateaux and trifle.

Cross-contamination

Cross-contamination happens when something in the kitchen, like a dish cloth, knife or chopping board, transfers poisonous bacteria from raw food onto high risk food. For example, by using the same knife and board for cutting raw chicken and then cooked ham, without thorough disinfection between each task.

Cross-contamination is a very common cause of food poisoning, but you can help to prevent it by having a high standard of kitchen cleanliness, and by always keeping high risk food in the refrigerator. Using different coloured chopping boards, and separate knives, for raw and cooked food, is another useful safeguard.

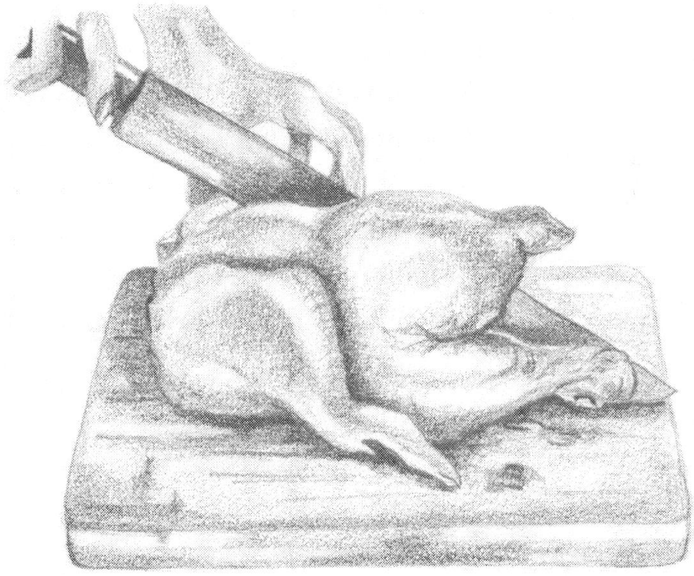

Using the same knife and board for raw and cooked meat can cause cross-contamination

Reheating

Reheated food is a common cause of food poisoning, especially when the food was not cooked or handled properly in the first place. It is important that food is reheated to a temperature of at least 75°C in the centre or thickest part, to destroy any bacteria that might be present. Food should not be reheated more than once.

Hot holding

Food to be eaten hot should be served as soon as possible after cooking. When food has to be kept hot for a while, it must be held at a minimum temperature of 63°C. This is because bacteria cannot reproduce at this temperature. Food that is being kept hot should be frequently tested with a thermometer probe to make sure the core temperature stays above 63°C.

Storage of dry food

The correct storage of food is extremely important. If there is a dry goods store, it should be kept clean and tidy. High protein food, such as packet soups and milk powder, must be kept completely dry, or they could become a food source for bacteria. All dry food should be stored in suitable containers to prevent contamination by insects.

Refrigerators

A refrigerator should run at between 0°C and 5°C. High risk and perishable food should always be stored under refrigeration. This is because most food poisoning bacteria, and those bacteria that cause food to 'go off' reproduce more slowly at low temperatures.

All food should be covered, and raw meat should be stored in a container on the bottom shelf of the refrigerator so there is no chance of meat juices dripping onto other foods.

Freezers

A freezer should run at between -18°C and -21°C. Bacteria are dormant at these temperatures so cannot reproduce. Frozen raw meat should always be thawed in a covered container, preferably in a refrigerator, well away from high risk food.

It is safer not to cook poultry without thawing it first. If you cook a chicken that is still frozen, the outer meat of the breast and thigh might be fully cooked, while the inner part of the bird is still relatively cool, well below the temperature needed to kill any bacteria.

The temperature of refrigerators and freezers must be checked regularly with a thermometer to make sure they are working properly.

Personal hygiene

People who handle food must maintain the highest standards of personal hygiene. Food poisoning is often caused by someone handling food without washing their hands. You must always wash your hands before starting work in the kitchen, and after any task that could contaminate them, for example:

using the toilet
blowing your nose
handling raw food
using chemicals
handling waste food.

Hair and dandruff must be prevented from falling in the food. If hairnets are not worn, it is very important that anyone with long hair has it tied back off their face and shoulders.

Fingernails should be kept short so that no dirt is trapped. Nail varnish should not be worn, as it might chip off into food. Harmful bacteria are found in cuts, boils and septic spots, so they must always be covered by a waterproof dressing.

Clothing

Anyone handling food should wear clean clothing made of a smooth material that is unlikely to trap dirt and bacteria. An overall is the best choice for working in a kitchen, as it helps to protect food from any bacteria that might be on your clothes.

It is advisable not to wear jewellery in the kitchen. A small piece of jewellery coming loose and falling into the food could harm someone if swallowed. Apart from food safety concerns, metal necklaces and bracelets conduct heat surprisingly quickly and can easily burn the skin.

General health

No one suffering from sickness or diarrhoea should handle food. No one should handle food if a member of their household or a close personal contact has symptoms of food poisoning. It is also unwise for someone with a bad cough or cold, or an ear, throat or skin infection to handle food. If in doubt, it is safer to take medical advice than risk causing food poisoning.

Training in food safety

When a premises is used to prepare and serve food to the public on a regular basis, it must be inspected by an officer from the Department of Environmental Health. They will check that the appropriate controls are in place to ensure the food is safe to eat.

Even if you are not running a food business, if you are handling food outside the home it is advisable to have some training in food safety. This applies whether you work as a volunteer, or in paid employment. Training will lessen the chance of food being exposed to the risk of contamination. It also gives you confidence that the food you serve has been handled correctly and is safe to eat. The Environmental Health office, at your local authority, should have a list of training centres in your area.

How to prevent accidents in the kitchen

Accidents are more likely to happen in an unfamiliar kitchen than at home. The chance of an accident increases when people are working closely together, handling large and heavy pans, and are under pressure to produce a meal on time.

A good first step towards preventing accidents in the kitchen is to wear suitable clothing. A long sleeved overall will help to protect your arms from burns and scalds. If the sleeves are close fitting, they cannot get caught on equipment or pan handles. Solid shoes with non-slip soles will protect your feet and lessen the chance of slipping on a wet floor.

Falls

Many accidents in the kitchen are the result of people falling. The floor should always be kept clear of anything that could be tripped over. Someone carrying a loaded tray is especially vulnerable. They are unlikely to notice a small object lying on the floor in front of them, and if they do trip over it, they do not have a free hand to steady themselves. Loose mats that slide on the floor are also a hazard.

A slippery floor can cause an accident. It is a good rule to immediately wipe up anything that has been spilt on the floor. Spillages of grease and oil are especially dangerous. They are very slippery, difficult to see and not easy to remove. Kitchen paper spread over the remains of an oily spill will help to absorb the residue and make the floor less slippery. It will also act as a warning to people to be careful where they walk.

Cuts

Most injuries involving cuts come from sharp knives which have been handled carelessly. Knives should only be used for their proper purpose, stored safely, and washed on their own, rather than in the sink with the other washing up.

It is difficult to cut food safely on a chopping board that is sliding about on the work surface. Putting a non-slip mat, or damp cloth under the board, will help to keep it in place.

It is unsafe to try to cut meat or fish that is still frozen, as the knife can easily slip, causing an injury.

Burns

To help prevent burns you need enough oven gloves, or very thick cloths, for all the hot jobs in the kitchen. Tea towels are not substantial enough, and some of the domestic sized oven gloves which are joined together by a strip of material are too small for large roasting tins.

Wet cloths conduct heat very quickly. Any oven cloth that is not completely dry should be discarded immediately in case someone uses it by mistake.

When removing hot tins from the back of the oven, the best protection against burns is a pair of extra thick elbow length oven gloves. It is a good rule not to take hot roasting tins out of the oven unless there is a suitable work surface nearby to put them on.

Scalds

People can easily get scalded when reaching over hot saucepans. If possible, pans that need attention during the cooking time should be put on the front rings of the cooker. Pan handles should not be placed over a heat source, or left sticking out from the cooker.

Large heavy pans full of vegetables and boiling water are a potential hazard. When the vegetables are cooked and ready to be drained, it is safer to bale out some of the boiling water before carrying the pan to the sink. Heavy pans should be carried by two people, and everyone else warned to keep out of the way. To prevent scalding as the steam escapes, you should always raise the pan lid first on the far side, away from your face, see 'Straining vegetables' *(page 70)*.

Never put a container of hot liquid up on a high shelf to cool. Someone could reach for it, thinking it was empty, and get badly scalded.

Accidents with electrical equipment

Electrical gadgets should be in good working order, well maintained, and used with care. It is safer not to carry on a conversation with someone who is using an electrical gadget, in case they are distracted and lose concentration. The instructions for all electrical gadgets should be kept together in an easily accessible place.

First aid

However careful you are, unfortunately, accidents will still occur, so there needs to be a well stocked first aid kit near at hand. A simple guide to basic first aid techniques can also be useful, along with a list of emergency telephone numbers, just in case there is a more serious accident.

Kitchen equipment and utensils

When deciding to buy kitchen equipment, you will obviously be influenced by the type of meals you serve, and the number of people you cater for. There will probably be financial considerations as well. When choosing large items of equipment, it is important to take into account the layout of the kitchen. If it is necessary to remove a section of work surface to accommodate the new equipment, be cautious. You can never have too much work surface when catering for large numbers.

The internet has details of dozens of suppliers, selling both new and second-hand catering equipment. There are also specialist kitchen shops which carry a large range of smaller gadgets and utensils.

Large equipment

Bain marie – a bain marie is extremely useful if you are regularly catering for large numbers. There are various sizes and styles to choose from, including some which have a heated cupboard for plates. A bain marie that is big enough to hold meat and vegetables for a large dinner will take up a lot of space and be very expensive to buy.

Cooker – this must be large enough for big pans and roasting tins and have at least six rings. Do not be tempted to buy two small cookers instead of one large one. The rings and ovens will be far too small. It is useful to have a grill, either as part of the cooker, or as a separate piece of equipment.

Dishwasher – a domestic dishwasher will probably be too small, and certainly too slow for large quantities of crockery. Some commercial dishwashers only take a few minutes to complete a cycle, but they are very expensive.

Freezer – a chest freezer takes up more floor space than an upright freezer, and is difficult to keep tidy, although the top can double up as a temporary work surface. If the kitchen is only used once a week or so, a fridge/freezer will probably be adequate.

Microwave – a microwave is not essential when cooking for large numbers, but is very useful for heating up vegetarian dishes, baby food and plated meals for late-comers.

Potato peeling machine – in a busy kitchen which caters for a large number of people, a potato peeling machine saves hours of tedious work. However, a large machine needs suitable plumbing and drainage, and is expensive to buy.

Refrigerator – a refrigerator is essential, and if there is space, it is worth buying a large one and getting some extra shelves for it. It should be positioned so the door can be opened wide and you can get rectangular trays in and out without tipping them up. If there is not a separate freezer, it is worth considering a fridge/freezer.

Trolley – trolleys are useful when there are lots of tables to prepare and clear. They also provide temporary storage for plated meals.

Water boiler – this is a necessity, and should be a suitable size for the number of guests. The models that are permanently plumbed in are very efficient.

Small equipment and utensils

With small electrical gadgets it can be more satisfactory to have several individual ones that are specifically designed for their own particular job, rather than one machine that attempts to do everything. All gadgets in the kitchen should be simple, well made and easy to clean.

If you are involved in setting up a kitchen, be wary of letting well-meaning people give you unwanted bits and pieces from their own kitchens. Some donated items will probably be very acceptable, but only if they are suitable for your needs.

The following list includes a wide selection of smaller equipment, gadgets and utensils likely to be of use in the kitchen. Some are essential, some you can do without. It all depends on what you are cooking.

Apple corer – this little tool is of limited use, but great for preparing baked apples!

Baking trays – baking trays have many uses in the kitchen, and because of their shallow sides, the heat of the oven can quickly reach the food.

Bottle openers – it is worth having several openers, as they are easily lost.

Bowls – it is useful to have a selection of different sized bowls, and if they stack inside each other it helps with storage. Large mixing bowls can be used for washing lettuce and holding vegetables prior to cooking. A polypropylene 2ltr measuring jug, with its curved sides, graduated markings and comfortable handle, can be used as a small mixing bowl.

Butter curler – some butter curlers seem to work better than others, but the only way to find out is to try them.

Cake tins – apart from cakes and pastries, cake tins can be used for other things, for example:
Loaf tins for home-made pâté.
Bun tins and muffin tins for individual Yorkshire puddings.
Spring clip tins for cheesecakes.

Carving board – this should be big enough to take a large joint. If you carve with an electric knife, a wooden board is more suitable than a metal one. The blades of the knife cutting against a metal board make a very unpleasant noise.

Cheese cutting board – this simple gadget slices large blocks of cheese quickly and neatly. Replacement wires can be bought separately.

Cherry and olive stoner – this worthwhile gadget removes the stones from most cherries and olives, without altering their shape and appearance.

Chopping boards – it is useful to have several chopping boards, and they should be a suitable size for the amount of food being prepared. Different coloured boards for raw and cooked food will help to prevent cross-contamination *(page 127)*. It is more hygienic to store chopping boards in a rack on the work surface where air can circulate, than piled up in a cupboard or drawer.

Colanders – large colanders are essential when you need to wash, strain or steam vegetables. They should be wide enough to sit firmly across the top of a big saucepan, so they can also be used to keep vegetables hot. One or two domestic sized colanders can also be useful, but avoid plastic ones which soften over heat and are not very robust.

Egg slicer – this will cut a hard boiled egg into thinner slices than you can manage with a knife.

Electric knife – this is an excellent gadget for slicing joints of meat, loaves of bread, pasties and pies.

Foil dishes and roasting tins – these can be very useful when you are short of dishes or tins. If you are planning to use a foil tin for roasting a large joint, buy the strongest you can find, and support it on a baking tray.

Food processor - a good food processor can do a variety of tasks including chopping and slicing, saving hours of tedious work. However, it can be an expensive gadget to buy. Food processors also vary greatly in their level of performance and in how much food they can deal with at one time. Do plenty of research before buying one.

Frying pans – a couple of solid frying pans and an omelette pan are likely to be useful from time to time.

Garlic press – this crushes cloves of garlic quicker than a pestle and mortar, although it is rather fiddly to clean.

Grater – a good choice is a metal 'box' grater with four different grating surfaces.

To grate orange or lemon rind with minimum wastage, place a piece of greaseproof paper between the fruit and the grater. As the rind is grated, the zest will collect on the paper and can be easily scraped off.

Kettle – a small kettle that will boil up quickly is essential to keep the workers happy! If the water boiler is not large enough for the number of guests, you also need a large kettle.

Knife sharpener – to keep knives sharp.

Knives – the following selection will tackle most everyday jobs in the kitchen:

Cooks knife with a blade 15cm to 20cm (6in to 8in) long for general chopping and slicing. Choose one that is comfortable to hold and not too heavy. It can also be useful for cutting and serving a gateau, and is a more suitable width than a pie server.

Serrated bread knife.

Carving knife (and fork).

Two or three serrated general purpose knives with blades about 12cm / 4½in long, including one with a very thin blade.

Two small vegetable knives with blades about 8cm / 3¼in long.

Grapefruit knife.

Palette knife.

Knife with a slightly flexible round ended blade for spreading butter.

Ladles – you need ladles for dishing up soup and stew. A catering ladle will usually have a measurement etched on the handle. These measurements are not always accurate, so if the size of the ladle is important, it is better to check it yourself.

Lemon squeezer – one that separates the pips from the juice is best.

Liquidiser or blender – a time saving gadget, especially when making soft breadcrumbs and home-made soup. Choose one with a large goblet that takes apart for cleaning.

Measuring jugs – measuring jugs of 2ltr / 3½pt capacity are the most versatile. It is also worth having a 500ml jug for measuring smaller amounts of liquid.

Measuring spoons – these are ideal of measuring out small amounts of herbs and seasoning. Spoons that give both metric and imperial measures can be used for any recipe.

Melon ball scoop – the ones with a different sized scoop at each end are best.

Mixer – a mixer is very useful for whipping cream and egg whites. It should work at variable speeds and have a large bowl. A mixer that can be taken apart and used as a hand held whisk is often useful.

Ovenproof dishes – dishes about 5cm / 2in deep are the right depth for meat pies and hot puddings. You may need some single serving ovenproof dishes if you make any individual meals.

Pastry brushes – these come in varying widths. Synthetic bristles are easier to keep hygienically clean than natural ones.

Pastry cutters – useful for making decorations as well as biscuits and tartlets. A set of round cutters of different sizes, that fit together for easy storage is a good choice.

Piping bags – it is worth having two large piping bags with matching star nozzles. One can then be in use while the other is being refilled. Small disposable piping bags are ideal for messy little jobs, like piping melted chocolate.

Pizza wheels – they make a neat job of cutting pizzas into slices.

Potato masher – a catering sized masher is best for the initial mashing of a large quantity of potato. A domestic sized masher is good for breaking up any little lumps that remain. Some small potato mashers have uncomfortable handles – try before you buy!

Potato peelers – there are at least three different styles of hand held potato peeler, and most people have a preference. It is so easy to throw a potato peeler away with the peelings that it is a good idea to have a couple of spares.

Roasting tins – having several different sized tins will give you more flexibility when you are trying to make the best use of the oven.

Rolling pin – apart from rolling out pastry, a wooden rolling pin with flat ends is good for crushing biscuits for a cheesecake base.

Salad spinner – this is a good gadget for removing excess water from washed lettuce. Those without holes in their outer casing can be used on a work surface.

Saucepans – if you are cooking a large number of hot dinners, you will probably need at least:
four large pans – for vegetables, soup and stew
two medium sized pans – for gravy and custard
one or two small pans
one non-stick milk pan.

Any pan that is used for soup or stew should have a heavy base to reduce the likelihood of food sticking or burning on the bottom. Except for the small milk pan, they should all have well fitting lids. The size of the pans will obviously depend on how many people you are catering for.

As a guide for 50 people:
For vegetables, soup and stew – 20ltr saucepan about 38cm / 15in across and 25cm / 10in deep.
For gravy and custard – 8ltr saucepan about 25cm / 10in across and 18cm / 7in deep.

Scissors – one or two pairs of general purpose kitchen scissors are essential. Small pairs of scissors with thin blades are useful for fiddly jobs, like cutting profiteroles, or sprigs of parsley. If you use banquet roll, battery operated scissors are worth having. Alternatively, use a pair of large scissors with straight blades.

Servers, turners, lifters, slices – these come in a variety of styles and sizes. The following selection will cover most jobs in the kitchen:
Small plain rectangular or square server, for dishing up pies and crumbles that have been made in straight sided dishes or tins. Also good for dishing up stuffing balls.
Larger rectangular slotted server, for dishing up roast vegetables and sausages. The slots allow fat to drain back into the tin.
Long rectangular server, for lifting fish and oblong plaits.
Pointed pie server, for serving large cakes, round pies and flans.

Serving spoons – a large plain serving spoon is always useful in the kitchen. A perforated serving spoon is good for dishing up vegetables on to individual plates. A vegetable or chip scoop, which is larger, is quicker if you are dishing up into serving dishes.

Sieves – a large sieve that is wide enough to stay in place across the top of a saucepan or mixing bowl is useful for removing excess liquid from stews, or fragments of bone from meat stock. You will also need several smaller sieves, and perhaps a tiny one for sprinkling icing sugar or paprika.

Spatulas – flexible rubber ended spatulas come in various sizes, and are the best utensil for scraping out bowls, jugs and blender goblets. A rubber spatula with a spoon shaped head (called a 'spoonula') is the right shape for scraping whipped cream out of a large bowl and into a piping bag.

Thermometers – fridge and freezer thermometers are necessary from a food safety aspect. A digital thermometer with a probe is essential for the accurate checking of cooking temperatures. If the probe is attached to a lead it gives more flexibility. A container of anti-bacterial probe wipes should be kept in the kitchen for disinfecting the thermometer probe.

If the cooker is rather unreliable, an oven thermometer can also be useful.

Timer – a simple timer has saved many a dish from disaster!

Tin openers – if you need to open a number of large tins quickly, a commercial sized tin opener is worth having. Otherwise, a couple of strong, hand held tin openers will be adequate.

Tongs – they are very versatile and it is worth having several pairs in different sizes. At a buffet, tongs are useful when people are serving themselves to things like chicken legs and salads.

Weighing scales – if you are catering for a large number of people it is worth having two weighing scales. One for vegetables and heavy joints of meat, and a smaller one for normal use.

Whisks – these come in various sizes and it is useful to have a selection. A strong metal whisk is better than a wooden spoon for mixing large quantities of packet soup or custard. For this job, choose a whisk with a long handle, so it cannot slide down and disappear in the soup.

Wire cooling trays – even if you are not making cakes in the kitchen, wire cooling trays are useful for cooling pastries, desserts and Yorkshire puddings.

Wooden spoons – it is important to have a good selection of wooden spoons, including one or two with long handles to use in large pans.

Zester – this is an efficient little tool for removing thin strips of zest from citrus fruits. It is quicker and less messy than a grater.

Miscellaneous items

Baskets and wooden bowls – they are good for presenting a variety of food, including crisps, bread rolls, baked potatoes and fruit. They also make attractive containers for small gifts and novelties. If you are eating outside, baskets are especially useful, being light to carry and virtually unbreakable.

When a wicker basket is used for food, the inside should be lined with a clean white napkin, a waiting cloth or doily. Baskets made from washable, synthetic materials are suitable for direct food contact.

Containers – square and rectangular containers are the best shape for fitting into a refrigerator. Containers that will stack together when empty will save space.

Doilies – these come in various shapes, sizes and patterns, and are great for giving instant 'added value' to a dish.

Food covers – the small circles of muslin weighted with beads will help to protect milk jugs and sugar bowls against insects. A 'food umbrella' will keep flies off larger food items, providing the edges of the umbrella are in contact with the table or work surface. Cheap plastic mixing bowls and disposable salad bowls, turned upside down, can be used instead of cake domes to keep flies off plates of food.

Instruction booklets – the instruction booklets for electrical equipment should be kept in a convenient place, and people working in the kitchen should know where to find them.

Oven gloves – you need several pairs of oven gloves, or special cloths, for the various hot jobs in the kitchen. A pair of thick, elbow length oven gloves, from a catering supplier, will help to prevent burns when removing hot tins from the back of the oven.

Trays – large, rectangular, non-slip trays are the best for general use. If they are all the same shape and size, they will stack together for easy storage. If the trays fit in the refrigerator you can 'tray up' cold starters and desserts and keep them cool.

Small, non-slip trays that can be easily carried in one hand are useful for clearing glasses.

Waiting cloths – use them when you are pouring coffee at the table, or carrying hot dishes. They look much smarter than oven cloths. If there are no waiting cloths, white tea towels are a good substitute.

Apart from cooking equipment and utensils, you might need some greaseproof paper, kitchen paper, foil or cling film. A large waste bin, lined with a strong plastic sack is normally the best solution for kitchen rubbish, with another bin for recycling waste. Somewhere in the kitchen there should be a bin where wet or dirty kitchen cloths can be discarded.

At a large dinner you need a good supply of dish cloths and tea towels. Scrapers and scourers are useful for washing very soiled items. Some of the scourers made from thin, twisted strands of metal can break up after a while, so it is important to replace them regularly. Materials for washing up and keeping the kitchen clean are just as important as the correct equipment for preparing and cooking the meal.

Fresh produce - how much do you need?

Unless it says to the contrary, all recipes in this book are based on produce that is 'prepared' weight. This is the weight that remains after any necessary peeling and trimming.

The following table gives an idea of the weight of usable fruit or vegetable that is left after preparation. It is shown as a percentage of the total unprepared weight, and should make it easier to calculate how much produce to buy for a large dinner. If the fruit or vegetables are very blemished, there will obviously be more wastage.

For example: you need 6kg of peeled and trimmed carrots. 80% of a carrot is usable and 20% is wasted in peeling and trimming. Therefore, to calculate the unprepared weight you need to buy, divide 6kg by 80 and multiply by 100 which gives 7.5kg.

If the carrots did not require peeling, but only trimming, then 90% is usable. In this case divide 6kg by 90 and multiply by 100 which means you need to buy 6.6kg of carrots.

Produce	**Preparation**	**Usable weight remaining after preparation**
Apples	peeled and cored	70%
Apricots	stoned	95%
Avocados	peeled and stoned	75%
Bananas	peeled	60%
Beetroot (fresh with leaves)	cooked and peeled	50%
Broccoli	trimmed	80%
Brussels sprouts	trimmed and any coarse leaves removed	65% - 80% (small sprouts are more wasteful)
Cabbage (green varieties)	core trimmed away and outer leaves removed	80%
Cabbage (hard white and red varieties)	core trimmed away and outer leaves removed	85%
Carrots	peeled and trimmed trimmed (not peeled)	80% 90%
Cauliflower (small)	trimmed and leaves removed	50% (there is less wastage with a large cauliflower)
Celery	trimmed	90%

Produce	Preparation	Usable weight remaining after preparation
Cherries	stoned	80%
Courgettes	trimmed	95%
Grapefruit	peeled	35% - 50%
Grapes	removed from stalks if necessary	95% - 100%
Kiwi fruit	peeled	80%
Leeks (partially trimmed)	remaining green part and ends trimmed	80% (there is 50% wastage if the leeks are bought untrimmed)
Mangoes	peeled and stoned	75%
Marrows	peeled and central core removed	70%
Melon	peeled and pips removed	65%
Mushrooms	stalks removed	90%
Nectarines	peeled	75%
Onions	peeled	95%
Oranges	peeled	40% - 65%
Parsnips	peeled and trimmed trimmed (not peeled)	85% 90%
Peaches	peeled and stoned	75%
Pears	peeled and core removed	75%
Peppers	stalk and core removed	80%
Pineapples	peeled and core removed	50%
Plums	stoned	85%
Potatoes (small)	peeled	80%
Potatoes (large)	peeled	90%
Raspberries	nil	100%
Spring greens	stalk and coarse outer leaves removed	50% - 75%
Strawberries	hulled	95%
Swedes	peeled	85%
Tomatoes (loose)	nil	100%
Turnips	peeled	80%

Conversion charts

Weight conversion chart – approximate equivalent

Grams	Pounds/Ounces
5g	¼oz
10g/15g	½oz
20g	¾oz
25g	1oz
40g	1½oz
50g	2oz
70g	2½oz
85g	3oz
100g	3½oz
120g	4oz
140g	5oz
150g	5½oz
170g	6oz
200g	7oz
225g	8oz
250g	9oz
300g	10½oz
310g	11oz
350g	12oz
375g	13oz
400g	14oz
425g	15oz
450g	1lb
500g	1lb 2oz
550g	1lb 4oz
600g	1lb 5oz
650g	1lb 6oz
700g	1lb 8oz
750g	1lb 10oz
800g	1lb 12oz
850g	1lb 14oz
900g	2lb
1kg	2lb 4oz
1.5kg	3lb 6oz
2kg	4lb 8oz
2.5kg	5lb 10oz
3kg	6lb 12oz

Liquid conversion chart – approximate equivalent

Litres	Fluid Ounces/Pints
5ml	1 level teaspoon
7.5ml	1 level dessertspoon
15ml	½fl oz / 1 level tablespoon
30ml	1fl oz / 2 level tablespoons
50ml	2fl oz
75ml	3fl oz
100ml	3½fl oz
125ml	4fl oz
140ml	5fl oz / ¼pt
175ml	6fl oz
200ml	7fl oz
225ml	8fl oz
250ml	9fl oz
280ml	10fl oz / ½pt
300ml	11fl oz
350ml	12fl oz
375ml	13fl oz
400ml	14fl oz
425ml	15fl oz / ¾pt
450ml	16fl oz
480ml	17fl oz
500ml	18fl oz
530ml	19fl oz
550ml	20fl oz / 1pt
700ml	1¼pt
850ml	1½pt
1ltr	1¾pt
1.1ltr	2pt
1.4ltr	2½pt
1.7ltr	3pt
2ltr	3½pt
2.2ltr	4pt
2.5ltr	4½pt
2.8ltr	5pt
3ltr	5½pt
3.4ltr	6pt
3.7ltr	6½pt
4ltr	7pt
4.2ltr	7½pt
4.5ltr	8pt
4.8ltr	8½pt
5ltr	9pt

Length conversion chart – approximate equivalent

Centimetres	Inches
5mm	¼in
1cm	½in
2cm	¾in
2.5cm	1in
3cm	1¼in
4cm	1½in
5cm	2in
6cm	2½in
7cm	2¾in
8cm	3¼in
9cm	3½in
10cm	4in
12cm	4½in
15cm	6in
17cm	6½in
18cm	7in
20cm	8in
23cm	9in
24cm	9½in
25cm	10in
30cm	12in

Oven temperatures

Very cool	110°C	225°F	gas mark ¼
	130°C	250°F	gas mark ½
Cool	140°C	275°F	gas mark 1
	150°C	300°F	gas mark 2
Very moderate	170°C	325°F	gas mark 3
Moderate	180°C	350°F	gas mark 4
	190°C	375°F	gas mark 5
Moderately hot	200°C	400°F	gas mark 6
Hot	220°C	425°F	gas mark 7
	230°C	450°F	gas mark 8
Very hot	240°C	475°F	gas mark 9

Index